THE FUTURE IN YOUR DREAMS

Annabelle Shaw

word4word

Copyright © 2008 Annabelle Shaw

First published 2008 by Word4Word, Evesham, UK

All rights reserved. No part of this publication may be reproduced, stored in a retrieval system or transmitted in any form or by any means, electronic, mechanical, photocopying, recording, scanning or otherwise, without the permission in writing of the publisher.

CIP catalogue records for this book are available from the British Library.

ISBN 978-1-906316-09-9

Printed and bound by Cromwell Press

Contents

Foreword	v
About the Author	vi
Acknowledgements	vii
Introduction	1
Chapter I: The History of Dreams About the Future	7
Chapter II: Baby Dreams	21
Chapter III: Winning Dreams	31
Chapter IV: Previews of the Future	41
Chapter V: Warning Dreams	65
Chapter VI: Dreams of Death	69
Chapter VII: Telepathic Dreams	81
Chapter VIII: The Importance of Sleep	95
Chapter IX: Results of Research into Premonition Dreams	97
Appendix: Charts	111
Bibliography	117

Dedicated to

the memory of John H. Warner

Foreword

To Dream of the Future

To see into the future – is it a blessing or a curse? Can we really do it? Do we really want to?

These questions have intrigued mankind down the centuries and most people have some opinion on whether or not it is advisable to find out what lies ahead. I am a palmist and I usually find that most people, once they know what I do, will sooner or later say, 'Ok then, what can you tell me?'

I came to know Annabelle Shaw when she became a student on one of my courses at the Isbourne Holistic Centre, Cheltenham. She quickly showed that she could interpret signs and put them into meaningful messages for her questioners. She has gone on to do readings at events such as charity fund raising days, corporate and private parties and sales promotion nights.

That she has the ability in divination is not surprising given her experiences of having dreams that later replay in real life – events, people and places all come into her life that she has previously seen in her dreams.

This book contains accounts from a range of people who, like Annabelle, have had dreams which were premonitions of the future. Here we have fascinating stories of foreseeing gambling wins, journeys, births, people, accidents and a variety of other small and major events.

The reasons that we may see the future in our dreams are open to debate. The fact that people have done so however is well documented by Annabelle in these pages.

There is a saying, 'Be careful what you wish for – it may come true!'

The same may well be true about what you dream of. Sleep well!

John Edward

About the Author

Of Scottish and Scandinavian descent, Annabelle spent her formative years in Argentina, South America. Her family lived in Buenos Aires first of all, then moved to the country region of Tucumán, where many of the native Indian population and Mestizos (half-Spanish, half-Indian) lived. Her nanny was from a local Indian tribe, whose family worked on a sugar cane plantation. Annabelle's parents, both missionaries, paid for her nanny's education, so that she could have a city job later on if she so wished.

From an early age, Annabelle was surrounded by spirituality; most of her father's family were ministers, and the Latin American people who came to her father's church were intensely spiritual, in an emotionally free way. She soon found that there were two worlds: the world of the spiritually charged church and the night-time world of dreams, where strange previews of the future were shown. Annabelle also gleaned some ideas from her nanny, who believed in superstitions, ideas common in her own background.

Annabelle was educated in a private school in Argentina. At the age of four she was very impressed by her teacher, who seemed to bring out the best in everyone in the class! South Americans are flamboyant, and this pleased Annabelle, who would try to emulate them. No one can live in Argentina without noticing the beauty and splendour of nature; she was very impressed by her visits to the Amazon when her family went on outings.

Back in the UK, Annabelle and her sister went to a village school in Kilbirnie in Scotland, then Morgan Academy, Dundee, and later the University of Dundee where she studied English and Psychology. Annabelle still remains fascinated by the supernatural and by dreams in particular. She is currently writing an inspired novel.

Acknowledgements

I would like to thank all the people who filled in my questionnaire about dreams, and who have happily taken part in this book.

Thanks to my daughter for her encouragement and starting the project by putting a letter I had written to *Woman* magazine in the postbox, which reached fellow dreamers, much to my delight!

Thanks to my late husband John for reading the manuscript.

Thanks to the late John Warner, for his exuberance and for believing in me.

Many thanks to the University of Oxford, especially the staff at the Bodleian Library, for their assistance in my research.

The Society for Psychical Research, London.

Thanks to the Isbourne Holistic Centre in Cheltenham.

Thanks to Geoff from Geoff Cook's bookshop in Gloucester for his help in finding all the right books!

To Don Brooks for drawing up the charts.

To Dai Davies from Dursley, Gloucestershire for coming up with the great title *The Future in Your Dreams*.

Special thanks to Philip Berry for reading the manuscript and for his kind and thoughtful help in many ways.

Many thanks to all the staff at Word4Word, Evesham, in helping to materialise this book. And special thanks to a brilliant editor – Margaret Aherne.

This book has taken a while to come out. I actually started writing it some time ago! Since then I've experienced two bereavements, and although I believe in life after death, it is still difficult for those who have been left behind. I also found that I had to struggle with a couple of long-held ideologies, which came into question as a result of writing this book! But I feel that the book will bring comfort and confirmation to those who dream about the future. I hope this book will answer some of your questions; mysteries still remain, but what is life without a mystery or the quest to solve that mystery!

Lumen servamus antiquum

We preserve the ancient light

Introduction

This book will deal with people's dreams that come true. These dreams are drawn mostly from spiritual and supernatural experiences, from people who have genuinely had a preview of a future event when dreaming, rather than from a scientific angle, although some scientific research is included. Rather than the term 'precognition' I prefer to use the term 'premonition dreaming', which means having a preliminary view of a future event through one's dreams; these future-orientated dreams come through without any rational foreknowledge of a particular event. To me, premonitions are associated with natural psychics, whereas precognitions are associated with mental abilities – psychologists often use this term when studying psychic ability and brain functions. It is difficult to measure or quantify premonition dreams using purely scientific methods alone, because certain knowledge is, essentially, immeasurable.

I set out to write this book for two reasons: firstly because I have had premonition dreams, but was soon to discover that not many other people shared my experiences; and secondly I noticed that although there were a number of books on the market dealing with the interpretation of dreams, there weren't many on the intriguing subject of prophetic dreams. This led me to seek out fellow dreamers! I designed a questionnaire to see if there were any common links between people with this ability, and which aspects of life were most commonly previewed, if any. It seems there are some common personality traits shared by people who have premonition dreams. The premonition experiences fell into several categories, and I have entitled each chapter of this book accordingly. In them I have included the dreams and real-life events of people who kindly gave me their consent to publish their dreams in this book.

The Future in Your Dreams

The Wonder of Premonition Dreams

I advertised for dreamers in a women's magazine, so most of my respondents were women (though I know that the men also got to hear about it from their wives and work colleagues!). Originally, I chose a general-interest magazine as opposed to a psychic-type specialist one, because I wanted to see how many members of the public in general had premonition dreams. If I had advertised in a paranormal publication I might have received a bigger response, but then possibly a more biased one. I have included many of the responses of the readers of the magazine; I also collated various accounts of dreams by word of mouth, from both sexes. As mentioned earlier, several men encouraged by my research for this book have also participated. I have also included references to the many men who, throughout history, were famed for their premonition dreams; this was quite straightforward as the history books have more records of famous men than famous women! Research shows that, when asked to fill in questionnaires, in general only one third of modern men talk about their dreams, compared to two thirds of women.

The people who wrote to me were from all walks of life, and aged from fourteen years of age to eighty-nine. Many people's premonition dreams started at a young age or in their late teens, so it is clear that age, wealth, or status are not contributory factors to having this ability. Attitudes, however, are of great importance. Research by current parapsychologists suggests that those with warm, friendly and open personalities (extroverts) tend to have these dreams more than introverts, and this is reinforced by my own findings (see Chapter IX, 'Results of Research into Premonition Dreams'). Research also shows that those with the ability to think flexibly (i.e. who can view an argument from all sides) tend to be the same people who have premonition dreams.

I wondered if having a religious background may have been a factor, as some of the famous past and present-day seers have been born into families of ministers and pastors. However, according to my research, people who had premonition dreams (although being religious in the sense that 98 per cent went to church) tended to be quite open-minded about their beliefs and could be said to be more spiritually aware than religious. I would agree with the Rev. W. Mauleverer, who said in his book *Twelve Great Sayings of the*

Introduction

Mystics: 'what people want to know is the Truth'. He goes on to say that if a good Catholic speaks of that which we know in our hearts to be true, we do not all thereby rush off to become Catholics, or to accept any doctrines of which we are not sure. The same applies to other world views. My aim is to give an account of people's experiences and the possible reasons for prophetic dreams.

When reading the works of some people, it becomes apparent that they are torchbearers for the truth in spite of their religious persuasions and not because of them! Unfortunately, even today, some church members and ministers view premonition dreams with great suspicion; this stems from medieval superstitions, which have continued to the present day. Looking through a Bible Concordance or reading through the Bible should assure people that it does not say that having dreams about the future is wrong – quite the reverse is true, in fact (see Chapter I, 'The History of Dreams About the Future'). I have to say this because of some of the self-doubts which have been placed upon the shoulders of supernatural dreamers by those who have not actually experienced any of these dreams themselves. As Edgar Cayce (a former Sunday School teacher and later spiritual leader) is reported to have said: 'As one grows in virtue – [and] in patience – one will receive these gifts as a natural result.' His motto in life was 'Not self but others'. He had many premonition dreams as well as healing and perceptive abilities. He advised that 'In all of our seeking in these paths, ... we take on Christ's Consciousness for our protection and guidance. For above all else, the highest use of E.S.P. is to know ourselves to be His.' I would agree with that.

Professor Frederick Myers (University of Cambridge) founded the first society for psychical research in 1882. He believed that those who had gathered numberless experiences through many lifetimes were able to have divine-like abilities such as being able to see events before they happened. So the more spiritually evolved, the more likely one is to have premonition dreams.

There are a number of theories as to the cause of premonitions: for example, some say that dreams can come from a psychic source or from a spiritual source, from within ourselves or from an external source – the ancient Egyptians and the Jews, for example, believed that prophetic dreams came from God. Other factors (as mentioned earlier) point to an individual being psychic or sensitive enough to receive such information, so a person's psychological make-up and their personality play an important role. I have included other relevant information pertaining to premonition dream experiences in the following chapters.

How is it that people who have never met and are unrelated have written to me with similar dreams about a forthcoming event? Some people think that we have access to knowledge of the past, present and future in our dreams because when we sleep we can transcend the limits of time and are able to enter into a different dimension, thereby having an overview of all three states. Some theories suggest that we can time-travel in the astral realms; Einstein considered the possibility of time travel in his theory of relativity and said that if something was possible in the imagination then it was also possible in the real world. Other reports have been of messengers (angels) giving information to the dreamer in a pictorial and/or telepathic way.

No organisation has a monopoly on the truth; the spiritual experiences included in this book transcend cultural and religious backgrounds. The ability to dream about future events is a universal experience. It is irrespective of race, age, upbringing or religion. It is a gift or natural ability, just as the vocational gifts of music, art, writing and healing are. These talents come naturally to some people and not to others; some people can develop it, but most are born with it. Many of those who wrote to me were naturally talented and said that their experiences reinforced in them a belief in a higher order.

People can often tell a premonition dream from an ordinary dream because of certain characteristic signs, for example a particularly vivid life-like quality, and memory of the dream on awakening, followed by a lasting impression which stays in the mind just as any notable event would in the waking world. Those with a greater number of premonition dreams had other extrasensory and telepathic experiences generally and were more able to intervene in daily events as a result of a dream, thereby avoiding danger or a tricky situation. Of course, not all dreams allowed the possibility of action and were rather previews of a future event.

I believe that amidst all the hustle and bustle of life we can and do get a helping hand in mysterious ways: it's as if something is saying 'don't give up, there is a purpose, there is help from a powerful spiritual source'. Sometimes, looking at the vast number of people around, all the houses occupied, streets upon streets, it is

Introduction

easy to feel as insignificant as a grain of sand. It is encouraging to know that despite the numbers, despite the seeming anonymity, bewilderment and confusion, people are still receiving personal, specific and very relevant dreams which provide pointers. They seem to say: 'Don't worry, you're not alone and you are on the right track.' Or as an old lady I once knew, a very nice fortune-teller, Mrs Vernon, from Dundee in Scotland, used to say: 'What's afore ye will no' go past ye!', and I have found this to be the case! The following accounts of premonition dreams are accurate and true and many can be verified by others. (Some people wished to be known only by their initials for the sake of privacy.) I would like to say that my own dreams and experiences, no matter how strange they may seem, are also true accounts.

A lot of people wrote to me saying that they had found it reassuring to know they were not the only ones to have premonition dreams. So for all those who dream dreams that come true and for all those interested, this book is for you!

'You may say I'm a dreamer but I'm not the only one'

— *John Lennon*

Chapter I

The History of Dreams About the Future

One does not dream, one undergoes the dream.

Carl Jung

Where do precognitive/premonition dreams come from? People from the ancient empires believed that they came from two sources: either an external source, coming from God, spirit messengers, angels, deceased relatives and the like, or from an internal source – one's own insight, psyche, or soul.

The ancient Egyptian civilisations believed that Serapis, the god of dreams, could answer a dreamer's question or forewarn the dreamer of a coming event. Temples or 'dream centres' were set up throughout Egypt, each temple having a resident dream interpreter or Serapeum. I use the term 'dream centres' because from personal experience and the experience of others, there are clearly some areas of Britain that are more conducive to premonition dreams than others. I believe that the ancient Egyptians were also aware of this, hence the specific sites for their temples, where people could go along and sleep in order to induce dreams about the future (or have symbolic dreams which may have to be interpreted by the oracle/dream interpreter). Seeing a future event in a dream or receiving answers in a dream is still prevalent in the UK today, as shall be seen later. This belief in dreams helped Joseph the Israelite a great deal during his exile in Egypt, because the Egyptians did not scoff at Joseph's abilities. This brings us on to Biblical beliefs in dreams of the future.

I am including excerpts from the Bible in this book; there is still some misguided belief in certain churches that premonition dreams are from the devil, but this is not true. As you can imagine, this hostile attitude can be quite disturbing for people with a gift of prophecy or being shown events from the future. The people I have met who are intuitive in general are usually the opposite of what they are wrongfully being accused of. However, I admit that not all churches think like this. In truth, I just wanted to know where these negative ideas came from, and whether they were based on scriptural Truth. The result of this research showed that these beliefs did not come from the Bible, so where did they come from? The facts were quite enlightening: the ideas were designed by the church establishment and implemented in the fifth century (see below).

So now, I would like to include the familiar scriptural references to the type of supernatural events described in this book.

There are at least twenty-two references in the Bible to people receiving messages about the future via dreams; these messages came either from God or quite commonly from angels (the messengers of God). In the Old Testament, Joseph had the gift of interpreting symbolic dreams about the future. The Pharaoh raised Joseph to a position of great power and responsibility because of this extraordinary ability. While in jail, Joseph interpreted the dreams of Pharaoh's cupbearer and baker, who were concerned that no one was available to interpret their dreams. Joseph said, 'Do not interpretations belong to God?' (Genesis, ch. 40 v. 8). When the two cellmates had given an account of their strange dreams, Joseph informed the cupbearer that in three days he would be released and once again serve the king, but he told the baker that he would be executed after three days. Both these interpretations came true, of course. Even in his native land, Joseph had earned the name of 'master dreamer', having foretold his own destiny to his envious brothers. This ability came from God.

When Pharaoh had a dream, the whole of Egypt took an interest. They believed that the gods would speak to Pharaoh and to all royalty. The learned men and Pharaoh's magicians were puzzled by Pharaoh's dream of seven fat calves coming up from the river followed by seven lean cows, which then devoured the fat cows, but didn't look fatter for it. Joseph told him that the seven fat cows represented seven years of plenty for Egypt, which would then be followed by seven years of famine. Pharaoh decided there and then to put Joseph in charge of all the food stores in order to prepare for the difficult years ahead; he also made Joseph mayor of his palace, giving Joseph the signet ring from his own hand and then bedecking him in fine linen, robes and gold, because the spirit of God was truly with him, and Pharaoh counted himself very fortunate for meeting and believing in Joseph. History shows that both Joseph's and Pharaoh's attention to dreams saved Egypt from a time of famine.

The History of Dreams About the Future

In the New Testament we can see that Pontius Pilate, the Roman governor in charge of Jesus' sentencing, took heed of his wife's warning in a dream, and said 'I wash my hands of any judgement of this innocent man' (Matthew, ch. 27 v. 19); he then publicly washed his hands of the whole affair.

It is not really surprising that Pilate took note of his wife's dream, as the people of Rome were always hearing of omens and portents of the future, as well as paying heed to prophetic dreams. William Shakespeare wrote a play based on the true account of Julius Caesar's assassination. This Roman emperor was not liked by his government, who secretly plotted against him, in the interest (they believed) of the public. Caesar's wife Calpurnia had a dream that Caesar's life was in danger so she warned him not to go to the Senate House that day to receive the people. When Caesar confided this dream to his friend Marcus Junius Brutus (also one of the secret plotters and betrayer of Caesar) Brutus explained it all away, thus enticing Caesar to his fate. He was killed by conspirators on 15 March 44BC, a date known as the Ides of March.

In the second century AD, the Roman historian Suetonius collected and recorded many famous people's dreams. He recorded that Caesar Augustus had a great respect for and reliance upon dreams. A friend had once saved his life by telling him of a warning in a dream.

As in Egypt, both the Romans and the Greeks had incubation centres for dreams. The ancient Greeks originally built these centres for Asclepius (or Aesculapius, as he was known to the Romans), the god of healing. Visitors to the temple would request a dream from their god giving remedies for their complaints. Visitors whose requests in dreams had been successful erected testimonial plaques. Later on, dream interpreters recommending medicines on the content of dreams became more fashionable.

The great Greek philosopher Plato held that a person consisted of a body, a mind and a soul. The physical body would receive sense impressions from the material world. The mind would be interested in ideas, ideals or forms, and have the ability to see perfect forms. The soul was imprisoned within the body, but would be released at death in order to soar up into the perfect world of ideals in eternity: thus the soul had an eternal life. Like the Indian and Chinese people, the Greeks believed it was possible for the human soul to leave the body and visit a spiritual world inhabited

The Future in Your Dreams

by other spirit beings. Why was this a universal belief among people who had such different cultures? One reason might be that they all actually experienced it enough to write about it.

The ancient Chinese believed that the spirit of man lived inside the physical body. This spirit within was able to make temporary, nocturnal journeys out of the body. During this time, the spirit of the dreamer would be able to make contact with departed friends and family, returning to the body with impressions of these visits. The ancient Chinese would never awaken a sleeping person in case the sleeper found it disorientating to re-enter their body suddenly.

Artemidorus was an Italian physician in the second century AD. He spent most of his life collecting information about dreams. This information, gleaned from old manuscripts, visiting incubation centres and interviewing dream interpreters, was presented in a book entitled *Oneirocritica*, from the Greek 'oneiric', meaning dream. *Oneirocritica* actually consists of five different books, three about the meanings of dreams and two offering hints about how a dream interpreter should conduct himself. He also tried to improve his interpretations by studying the dreams of hundreds of individuals, classifying his findings into five categories: symbolic dreams, oracles containing divine revelations, fantasy dreams, nightmares and daytime visions (daydreams). Artemidorus' reputation suffered because of the commercial dream books that followed his – mostly dealing with various interpretations. The gypsies of the second century AD managed to retain powers in the interpretation of dreams but tended to put things into codes later, during the Spanish Inquisition, in order to protect themselves from persecution. Dreams and their meanings became a bit nonsensical to others and were therefore dismissed as superstitious mumbo-jumbo.

So why did the rest of the world accept premonition dreams as part of the normal world, but not the Christian Church?

Religiosity versus Spirituality

It is still possible to access spiritual truths within the organisation of Christianity. The best place to become spiritually aware within the Christian Church is probably in the Latin American churches or a church which is in touch with the spiritual side of Christianity, such as the American churches of African descent. These churches usually give one the opportunity of having a direct encounter with God, or a numinous experience. Many of the Catholic churches can be quite stirring too, especially those in the Charismatic movement, and it is possible to walk around on your own and tap into the beneficial energies there. Other churches (such as the Church of England) can offer us conformity and predictability, with ceremonies dating back to the seventeenth century. Visitors here can read the intelligently written church prayer book, *The Book of Common Prayer*. In this situation, meditating on the written word of the Church's ancient books can help. This type of church will be more accommodating to people who are intuitive outside of the Church.

In 1936 the Archbishop of Canterbury, Cosmo Lang, carried out a review of long-held church beliefs and found that having spiritualist abilities was not incompatible with the Bible. The Pentecostal type of churches believe in healing and prophesies, even in having prophetic dreams, but – and it's quite a big 'but' – only if it is compatible with church beliefs. This stems from an array of contrived beliefs from the fifth century, which I will discuss soon.

During the fifth century, the prophetic dreams of bishops and monks were considered divine and very favourable, whereas those of anyone else, that is lay people and villagers, were viewed with fear and suspicion. The great question was 'Where do these dreams come from?' One of the great thinkers, Thomas Aquinas (in the thirteenth century), postulated that only the clergy could have foresight into the future, being chosen by God to enter the ministry. This pious attitude seems strange, as angels would visit people from various backgrounds in dreams throughout the Bible. In fact, one would be hard pressed to find a bishop or a monk in the Bible – because there weren't any; they came along with the institutionalised Church, formed by the converted Christians within the Ancient Roman Empire. The 'church' leaders in the Bible were actually Rabbis, and later on they were travelling disciples, using a common purse, who went round healing the sick and preaching forgiveness.

Where did this deviation from the Biblical records come from, and why? Following on from the Roman Empire came the Roman Catholic Church, run by the same people (Roman Emperor/Pope); it was a continuation of the same power system, which incorporated the Christian doctrines following the conversion of the

The Future in Your Dreams

Roman Emperor, Constantine. The Catholic Church was, and still is, well known for assimilating ancient beliefs into its own, in order to attract and keep converts. For example, 31 October was originally a pagan festival called Salat (a day for remembering the dead); the Christian Church changed its All Saints Day (a day for remembering saints and martyrs throughout Christian history) from May to 1 November, and called it All Hallows Eve – Halloween. This was done both to replace pagan festivals and to incorporate new, yet familiar, festivals for new converts. After all, the Christian events still happened, only the dates were different. Later on, the protestants abolished All Saints Day because they didn't believe in saints or in the idolizing of saints, and so Halloween became a secular celebration as well as a Christian one.

The ancient English name for the Spring Equinox is Eostrata, celebrating a time of fertility symbolised by an egg. Easter time in the Church would fall on the first full moon after the Equinox, usually in April. The Easter egg and rolling of painted hard-boiled eggs would symbolise the rolling away of the stone from the tomb of Jesus. Incidentally, the Spring Equinox contains 12 hours of light and 12 hours of darkness: the number 12 is a very significant number in the Bible.

Usually, any ideas which could not easily be incorporated into the Christian belief system were suppressed or eradicated. Anyone holding other views were, and still are, called heretics. In AD 258 many of the early Christians were killed under orders from the Roman Emperor Valerian, and with them died some of the ancient Christian knowledge. Many of the original scrolls were burned. Before this time, it was acceptable for priests and monks to get married, but fear of the Christian Church's wealth being dissipated through inheritance to families led to this practice being altered; this was then backed up by the apostle Paul writing of the virtues of a single life.

In the fifth century, the Church rulers were very keen to streamline the Church. The Bible became standardised and any dubious or ambiguous material was pruned out. This was apparently done in order to reflect the true core beliefs of the early Church. Later, during the Middle Ages, fanaticism and, possibly, fear of losing control over the population led to a complete ban on talk of any supernatural phenomena. They then confiscated and kept any books or information gathered by people from various ancient belief systems; in Britain this would have included ancient pagan beliefs. A book by Brian Bates entitled *The Way of Wyrd* is quite an interesting book to read on this subject; although written as a novel, it is sourced from historical documents of the time.

As mentioned earlier in the chapter, in the thirteenth century Thomas Aquinas came up with a theory on dreams. According to him, dreams came from two sources: either from God, or from the Devil. Furthermore, he asserted that priests always had premonition dreams from God but anyone else had premonition dreams from the Devil! Since not many people had premonition dreams anyway, why would they object? The word 'devil' in the Bible (from the Greek *diabolos*) actually means 'adversary'. Interestingly, the word 'duvvel' is actually part of a gypsy phrase meaning 'God bless you'; people of that time (thirteenth century) understandably thought that 'duvvel' meant the opposite of the word 'God'. The gypsies, choosing not to mix with the locals, were misinterpreted, and their Romany language was rightly seen as some sort of secret code spoken amongst themselves. The image of the devil with horns comes from 'primitive' men (shamans) dressed up in antlers or horns for one of their harvest ceremonies.

The dreams which were approved of by the Church were, of course, the ones that were puzzling and muddled and that came from everyday things: the mind sifting through everyday events. This type of dreaming was acceptable, harmless enough, and so allowed. Other dreams, however, especially clear dreams that came true, prophetic dreams, had to be censored from the public domain. The best way to do this was to instil terror and distrust by hypothesising that premonition dreams came from the Devil. This idea became a belief, which became increasingly popular. Eventually, the idea of devils and demons came to play a progressively greater role in theorising about the origin of dreams. It was suggested that the Devil had many disguises available to him and could thus pass easily into a person's dreams. This problem was not confined to the Catholic Church, but appeared in all branches of Christianity. The protestant reformer Martin Luther had visions in dreams, but was so worried about them coming from Satan that he prayed for God not to speak to him through his dreams.

Absurdly enough, Thomas Aquinas used to believe in precognitive dreams too, and also in the power of magic. He would use some of these practices to his own advantage; for example, being a clever and studious person, he hated to be interrupted by the noise of passing horses with chariots. So, following a magical procedure, he made a small bronze statue of a horse and placed it underneath the road of the chariots, perhaps with some intent for silence thrown in. Then, Abracadabra, success! No more horses and chariots, instead, peace, perfect peace, and tranquillity.

As we shall see later, modern research into premonition dreams shows that the people who do actually have these dreams are kind, caring and humanitarian people who have either had a Christian background or are spiritually aware and would like to make the world a better place. In other words, enlightened beings.

A lot of people at the present time don't actually want to know about religiosity or spirituality; what they want to know about is their own truth. People have a great need now to be true to themselves and become who they were meant to be all along, before they were institutionally instructed and then bound by the constricting rules of various religions and education, if education is seen as teaching people to conform and obey in general. It is good to receive an education, but originally schools were designed partly to keep urchins off the street, and thereby become disciplined and reformed; the new wave is about finding one's own power. This path does not appeal, or even appear, to everyone; nevertheless: 'You shall know the truth, and the truth shall set you free' (John, ch. 8 v. 32).

There seems to be a distinction in the Bible between prophets and soothsayers or mediums. Both sets were gifted with foretelling future events, but only the Israeli prophets were to be accepted by the twelve tribes of Israel. During the Middle Ages the other two (fortune-tellers and mediums) came under the umbrella of witchcraft practices. While looking up the heading of witchcraft in the Biblical dictionary, I could only find the mention of Molech (also known as Moloch and Melek). In ancient times, there was a practice of 'walking through the fire', with reference to Molech; this was a ritual which involved sacrificing children to a Canaanite deity called Molech. Obviously the religious leaders were fiercely opposed to this, as were the Catholic Spaniards when they came across child sacrifices practised by the Incas in South America to please and appease their gods.

After the fifteenth century medieval musical instruments were taken out of the churches, along with beautiful art work and any ornaments that were considered idolatry. Martin Luther had defied both the Pope and the Emperor, wishing to free the Germans from Roman rule, but also wanting to translate the Hebrew/Greek version of the Bible into a new, European version; he did this excellently, but made one or two general interpretations which suited the people's education at the time. For example, in his time, Luther was tackled for mistranslating the names of animals:

> He explained that he did so only where it could in no way affect the sense of the passage and where an exact translation would mean absolutely nothing to anybody but a zoologist or philologist. A chameleon for instance might be a kind of elephant or snake for all the sixteenth century German knew to the contrary; so he felt justified in translating it as a 'weasel', which was an animal that meant something to his readers, even though a weasel is not a chameleon. (G. S. Wegner, *6000 Years of the Bible*, p. 210)

Having said that, a lot of the stories in the Bible are accurate and authentic, as they matched the stories in the ancient Dead Sea Scrolls which were amazingly found in an earthenware pot hidden in a cave by a shepherd boy, in the mid-twentieth century.

The Fifteenth to the Eighteenth Century

In the thirteenth century, Pope Gregory IX had ordered inquisitors to hunt for heretics, and in 1484 Pope Innocent VIII issued a bill confirming papal support for inquisitorial proceedings against witches. This bill was included as a preface to the *Malleus Maleficarum*, meaning 'The Hammer of The Witches', a book written by two Dominican inquisitors which was published in 1486. The book explained various colourful stories about what witches got up to, and helped to persuade public opinion that a cosmic plot, directed by Satan, threatened all Christian society.

As a result of the inquisitor's hunt for heretics, witches were to be rounded up in the towns and villages. In this atmosphere it is not surprising that premonition dreams would be kept mostly secret, known only to the dreamer. The ability to see into the future through one's dreams was, and still is, considered to be an 'Occult Science' (Neusner et al., *Religion, Science and Magic*).

The Future in Your Dreams

During the Middle Ages, the majority of women had little real influence in worldly affairs. However, many had expert knowledge of herbal lore, healing the sick and advising people about the future. These skills empowered women. Some would talk about omens and dreams, and what they meant. These were often put down as old wives' tales, but during the Inquisition they came under the sinister title of Witchcraft. 'Thou shalt not suffer a witch to live' was the favourite saying of the time. The word 'witch' meant having knowledge and supernatural powers that other people didn't have. During the Middle Ages, it was considered a sacred duty to rid the land of witches. Witches were the new 'out group'.

Fears of cosmic plots increased in periods of high social tension. The fifteenth and sixteenth centuries witnessed a widespread belief that the Antichrist was soon to appear, followed by the return of the Messiah, and that the transformation of the world was at hand. Later, in 1782, no fewer than 300,000 women suffered death in Europe, again because of accusations of witchcraft. In America, the infamous Salem Witch Trials of the late seventeenth century were carried out by the protestant Puritans. It is not surprising, then, that anyone with the gift of seeing into the future by having dreams or visions kept it quiet. True practitioners, such as Nostradamus, used codes and symbols. The witch craze was restricted to Europe and its colonies, where social unrest and sermons fuelled the craze in towns and villages.

Not only witchcraft, but also science, came under the repressive regime of the medieval Church. I think it was unfair, to say the least, that Galileo was prevented from speaking the truth by the Church authorities of the time. As we now know, Chinese astrologers discovered that the planets revolve around the sun; Galileo and some of the Church monks were also aware of this, but because Church doctrine taught that the earth was the centre of the universe and that the sun and the planets revolved around the earth, anyone saying anything to the contrary would have to be silenced. (After all, common sense would suggest that the sun did revolve around the earth; one only had to look up to the sky for confirmation.) We can see that this must have been a dilemma for the Pope. The truth of the matter came out two hundred years later, enough time to let the old beliefs die down and be replaced by the scientifically provable facts. Science changes according to

The History of Dreams About the Future

advancements whereas religious beliefs tend to be universal and unchanging. Things have moved on since then and the Vatican has its own observatory now.

Another interesting point, also discovered by the Ancient Chinese, was the astrological timing of Christ's birth. This was also backed up by the Persians and later by Galileo's contemporaries. On the nights of 10 and 11 October 1604 the astronomer Johann Brunowski, a pupil of Johann Kepler, noticed a new star shining with interchanging colours, much like a diamond. This was not a nebula or a comet. Kepler began to investigate the matter further by tracing previous planetary alignments. He noticed that the last time this configuration occurred was at around the time of Christ's birth. The configuration was as follows.

On 17 December 1603 there occurred a conjunction of the planets Saturn and Jupiter in the Zodiacal sign of Pisces in the watery trigon. In the following spring, they were joined by Mars in the fiery trigon, and in September 1604 there appeared at the foot of Ophiuchus and between Mars and Saturn a new star of the first magnitude. This star began to fade in March 1606. There is a conjunction between Jupiter and Saturn in the same trigon (Trine) every twenty years, but then they move into a different trigon every 200 years, and are not conjoined in the same trigon again until after a lapse of 794 years, 4 months and 12 days. By calculating backwards, Kepler discovered that the same conjunction of Jupiter and Saturn in Pisces had happened three times in the year 6 BC and that the planet Mars had joined them in the spring of 748. The general fact that there was such a combination at that time has been verified by several independent astronomers and astrologers. In the time of Christ's birth the Chaldaean astrologers knew that this event occurring in the constellation of Pisces meant that it would be connected to the fortunes of Judea. Myrrh and frankincense, two of the gifts brought by the magi to the infant Christ, are Arabian products, therefore it is likely that the magi were from Persia, home of the great mathematicians and astrologers. The early Church scholars Augustine and Chrysostom say that there were actually twelve magi, and that the figure three came about because of the three gifts. Much was made at the time of the three men bearing gifts representing the three stages of life – youth, middle age and old age, represented by Caspar, Balthasar and Melchior respectively.

The skulls of these three men can still be found among the relics of the Cathedral at Cologne.

The Twentieth Century and Beyond

At the turn of the twentieth century Freud brought dream analysis back, but put a medical emphasis on it, as a route to solving the mental problems of neurotic patients. In his book *Interpretation of Dreams* (1900), he described the dream as a medium for wish-fulfilment – a state in which one could explore one's needs and wishes, but if these needs and wishes were found to be unacceptable to the individual's conscious mind, they would become repressed and take on a symbolic form in the dream. Freud would then endeavour to translate the person's dreams in accordance with his own theories. This view tended to detract from, dismiss and trivialise premonition dreams, which did not exist in the scientific world as they could not be proved.

His contemporary Carl Jung, however, was a great believer in people interpreting their own dreams. He was not alone in this view, as shall be seen in later chapters. Some of Jung's sayings are worth mentioning: he said 'One does not dream, one undergoes the dream' and 'Consciousness can be trained like a parrot but not the unconscious'. Jung thought that one was not actually in control of the dream process.

Alfred Adler (1870–1930), the famous psychiatrist, thought that it was very important to bring dreams into the light of the waking world. He believed that symbolic dreams could help people to overcome either inferiority or superiority complexes. He also felt that it was important to make note of the emotions felt within the dream state so that people could benefit from this information in their day-to-day lives.

Jung believed in 'synchronisation' – for example, where unrelated people from distant places might invent similar machines at the same time, without ever having met. Inventors could do this, Jung believed, because they were in some way tuned in to the 'collective unconsciousness'. He also believed in archetypal figures in dreams that were common to all, and in general took a much more spiritual and open-minded view of dreaming. He believed it was best for the patient to interpret his or her own symbols, otherwise the dream would recur, representing the same unresolved problems. I personally believe in using lucid dreaming to stop recurring dreams or nightmares, for example shooting a lion, or menacing birds, that might be trying to harm you. It is best to become active in this type of dream rather than allowing it all to happen. I speak from my own experience: the dream I had was a symbolic version of a real-life situation. When I took charge in the lucid dream state (I shot a bird that was attacking someone) the traumatic situation in the real world actually reversed, to several people's benefit – in fact it was a life-saving reversal. This was a very important dream as it reoccured for three nights – the dream stopped when I shot the bird.

There are several mentions of angels giving messages to people in the Bible while awake and also through dreams. Recently there have been reports of visitations by angels even in this century! There are also other written accounts of people receiving messages through dreams. So we can see that despite the efforts of some scientists and religious groups, both past and present, visitations and premonition dreams still happen today. Why is this?

The reason for this is quite simple. The obstructions of the past – science and religion – were generated by materialistic worldly interests combined with intellectualism. But the power of the spirit of love (God is love) will continue to resist what are merely temporary ideologies to the contrary. Just as man-made physical structures cannot withstand forever the forces of the elements, so eternal truth will prevail. Hopefully we can return to true spirituality rather than religiosity. It is very sad to say that most churches started off being spiritually inspired but then became establishments once their founder member died. Having said that, there is a spiritual revival going on in the churches today, and the establishments (such as the Church of England) are reshaping themselves accordingly.

In the recent past, there has been an over-stressing of the material aspects of man and the nature of the universe but now, in the twenty-first century, a more spiritual and balanced attitude to life is emerging. There has been, and still is, a spiritual revival going on, not only in the churches but also in secular society. Doctors are taking note of patients' accounts of out-of-body experiences, as scientific technology is becoming more sophisticated. Many scientists believe that there is an underlying order in the universe which supports spiritual beliefs, that the world is not the result of chaos and evolution after all. There is work going on now, which would have once come within the realms of science fiction, about the possibility of time travel. The fact of premonition dreams invites questions as to the nature of time, the human psyche, life after death, and many others which I shall explore in greater detail in the following chapters.

Chapter II

Baby Dreams

An angel of the Lord appeared to Joseph in a dream saying . . . 'she [Mary] shall bring forth a son, and thou shalt call his name Jesus.'
Matthew, ch. 1 vv. 20, 21

Premonition dreams cover many aspects of life, from birth to death and all the events in between, so although these were not the most common experience, I shall start the records with dreams of new arrivals!

About 10 per cent of readers wrote to me of baby dreams. Many of these people had also dreamt of other subjects on other occasions (which will be covered in the appropriate chapters). This to me illustrates the importance of a child's arrival into the world, and also that it is a predestined event. In the Bible we read that Joseph had a dream in which an angel told him that Mary would bear a son, and that his name would be Jesus. Mary's cousin Elizabeth was also notified by supernatural means of the forthcoming birth of her son, John (the Baptist).

A lot of people dream of specific details regarding the new baby, such as whether it is a boy or a girl, the colour of hair or the time of arrival. Susan Jones from Witton in the West Midlands wrote:

> My friend Geraldine and I have known each other since we were five. When we left school, work and new friends let us see each other only occasionally, but we always tried to keep in touch.
>
> Throughout her pregnancy in 1993, I was adamant she was carrying a boy. Then at 4 a.m. on the 4th of September I woke up from a dream that she had given birth to a girl. We were all looking down at a beautiful baby. I couldn't really get back to sleep, and couldn't shake off the feeling I had. When I dressed in the morning, I rushed round to see Geraldine, just for peace of mind really, because the dream felt so real. I was shocked when I was told she'd given birth to a girl, Chelsea, at 4.06 a.m. When I saw Chelsea, she was exactly as I had dreamt, with her dark hair – everything.

The Future in Your Dreams

It was very easy for the women surveyed to recall their dreams, as premonitions always left a very strong impression on their minds. Mrs D. Willings of Suffolk says:

> I dreamed my sister's baby would be born on a Tuesday between midday and 1 p.m., and that it was a girl. She was born on a Tuesday at 12.30 p.m.!

Mrs Willings told me that her premonition dreams often come a few days prior to the actual event.

In our next dream, yet another preview is seen in vivid clarity. When she was five months pregnant, Mrs C. of London dreamt that her baby had red hair and that it would be a baby boy. She found this puzzling, as both she and her husband are dark-haired, yet the baby was indeed a boy, and he did have red hair!

Some people dream of gifts for their babies. For example, Mrs Y.B. of North Humberside wrote:

> When I was expecting my first baby, I had a cousin who visited very rarely – maybe once a year. In my dream, I was in the kitchen when a car pulled up outside, and in walked my cousin and her husband, carrying a brown paper parcel. She said it was a cardigan which she had knitted for the new baby. When I opened the parcel I found a really tatty cardigan.
>
> A few days later I was cooking dinner in the kitchen when my husband shouted through from the lounge that my cousin and her husband were pulling up outside. At first I thought he was joking, as I had told him about my dream, but sure enough, in they walked. My cousin was holding a brown parcel, just like in my dream. I was absolutely stunned, and at first I dared not open the gift. Eventually I did open it, and much to my relief, found a lovely white cardigan, perfectly knitted.

Some women dreamt of the date their new arrival would be delivered; for example, Mrs Taylor from London wrote:

> My third baby was due on the 1st of June. I didn't know the sex. Some weeks before, I dreamed that I was in hospital and I kept saying to the medical staff 'My baby must be born today, on the 23rd of May' – it was getting late and I dreamt I had a boy at 11.59 p.m.

Baby Dreams

Then on the 23rd of May I went into labour and our son was born just before midnight. I had told so many people about my dream that some rang up on the 23rd to ask me if anything had happened!

Jean Holland, who is a dream therapist and used to run dream workshops, wrote:

When I was living in Tewkesbury, England, I dreamed a friend of mine in Cape Town was holding a baby dressed in blue, which I took to mean it was a boy. My friend could not understand the dream, but within a few weeks her daughter discovered she was pregnant, and after having two girls she had a son. I had the same dream with my sister's first grandchild, and have dreamed that each of my cleaning ladies in South Africa have been pregnant before they knew themselves – and I dreamt of the due-date of their babies!

Mrs J. E. A. Kelly, an accounts clerk from West Sussex, wrote to me with several dreams. This one is about her cousin's baby:

I told my cousin I'd had a dream that she would have another baby. It was a girl. At that time she wasn't pregnant and hadn't even considered having another child. Three months later, my cousin became pregnant and bought some pink baby clothes knowing that my dreams always come true, and sure enough it was a girl!

Some women who wrote to me had been pregnant, but with reservations, until they had the following dreams. Mrs C.G. of Preston wrote:

In September 1994, I had just come back from my holiday in Spain with my fiancé, and was upset because I had just found out I was pregnant. My fiancé was happy about it, as it would be his first child, but I wasn't sure. Being a widow, and having brought up three sons by myself, I knew only too well what hard work babies are. I was thirty-eight, with three teenage boys – how would they react to the news? I faced a real dilemma: should I go ahead with the pregnancy or not?

I then had a dream that I was walking down a long road; everything was in black and white. In the far distance, I could just make out two silhouettes, one small, and one a large figure. As I got closer, everything turned into colour and I recognised my late husband. He was holding the hand of a small blonde-haired little girl, aged about two years. Over the next few weeks I had various dreams about my husband, always with this little girl. The only other person who knew about my pregnancy at this point, other than my fiancé, was my sister-in-law (my late husband's sister).

I told my sister-in-law about the recurring dreams I'd been having about her brother. She was a little taken aback, but wondered if my husband was trying to tell me that I was having a daughter this time, so not to have an abortion. I must admit I had thought the same thing. Anyway, after a lot of soul-searching, I decided to go ahead with the pregnancy. Everything went well with the pregnancy and birth, and to my delight, I gave birth to a beautiful baby daughter in May 1995.

When she was new-born, she had lots of very dark hair, but now that she is nearly a year old, she is completely blonde, and I am convinced that my late husband showed me a premonition.

The Bible and other religious scriptures (e.g. the Vedas) show that certain children are destined to be born to certain parents. Recently I have been reading a book entitled *Destiny of Souls*, by Michael Newton, in which people recall choosing their own parents before being born; then they were shown a preview of the salient points of their lives, and what their purpose in life was. Sometimes children didn't make it or lived for a short time only and Michael Newton explains in his books why this would be.

Mrs Smith had a dream telling her that her plans of having a family were not over yet!

> I was in hospital waiting for a sterilisation operation after the birth of our third son. I fell asleep one afternoon, something I never do normally, and I dreamt a very large black nurse told me not to have the operation as a little girl was in Heaven waiting for me to be her mum, and that I was needed for her and her for me. When I awoke I was so confused as to whether it had been a dream or real, but the duty nurse told me they had no such nurse on the ward. It all seemed so real that I could not go through with the operation. Five years later I gave birth to Hayley, who is very psychic. Even her birth date was unusual: 18–11–81, which reads the same forwards and backwards.

Apparently patients and nurses at St Thomas's Hospital in London have seen an apparition of a woman who tends to patients while they are asleep. The patients report having been visited by this person in a dream and then make a speedy recovery! Visits of this sort were widely reported during the Victorian era and are now reappearing. A friend who was staying overnight at my house in Carnoustie, Scotland (mentioned in Chapter IV), had a dream that his bed covers were ruffled, two elderly ladies came over to him and tucked him in, he felt comforted and continued to sleep. In the morning his bed was smoothed out and tucked in all round – he could not really have done this by himself, and looked a bit startled when he came down for breakfast and recalled his dream!

Dreams of Losing a Child Before Childbirth

> When a mother loses her child for whatever reason, I have found the odds are quite high that the soul of this baby will return again to the same mother with her next child. If this mother does not bear another child, the soul may return to another close member of the family because that was the original intent. (Michael Newton, *Destiny of Souls*, pp. 383–4)

Some people who answered the questionnaire said they were warned in dreams about miscarriages and forthcoming 'accidents'. Most of the messages from the premonition dreams were ignored, and the women went ahead and got pregnant anyway. In each case the mother-to-be subsequently miscarried or had to terminate the pregnancy. A lot of the women who had such dreams about their friends felt unable to pass the message on; they then felt guilty and in some way responsible. It is natural not to mention these types of dreams to people, partly because of the society we live in where certain subjects are still taboo, and partly because it is not considered good to be the bearer of such news before the event, just in case it doesn't happen. The very nature of individual personalities, dreams and opinions decrees that any one person can and will strive to be in control of his or her own destiny – they, and others involved, are usually responsible for their own actions.

In an ideal world, we would learn to act on all the premonition dream messages received, but this can only happen if we are not too strong-headed. In this way, the message is stronger, and not muted by the normal chattering censorship activities of the brain. This activity is an essential process which enables each of us to get through daily life without going round the bend because of the enormous amount of information we deal with every day. What I mean is that we ought to try and set aside some time each day in which to have a 'quiet time'. This is a very special part of each day when we can tune in to that still small voice that would otherwise be drowned out by our daily concerns. A lot of people find that things come to mind while going for a walk – this is the time when we are able to recognize influences in our lives that could otherwise be overlooked. I believe we are all capable of tuning in to the mysterious force which offers us insights! If you have a fleeting thought which seems not to fit in with what you're doing at the time, you can stop and say to yourself 'is this my own thought or is this an insight?' Examine the source or analyse how you feel about the information.

Some people felt that they could not act on a premonition dream as they were just watching a scenario of events, much like watching a preview to a movie. Some 99 per cent of people who wrote to me said that they could distinguish a premonition dream from an ordinary everyday dream, so as time goes by, and more and more of these dreams come true, we can learn to rely on that 'still small voice'.

Children's Dreams

Many of the people who dreamt about the future also had other supernatural experiences. Two experiences involved recollections from a childhood dream, set back in time.

Mrs P.C. from Cheltenham described a recurring dream from childhood:

> I am walking along a drive which leads me to a house, Georgian in appearance, double-fronted with an elegant pillared porch. I go through the door and stand in the spacious hallway. There is a sweeping stairway which ascends from both sides, curves and joins

a balustraded gallery running along the top. An alcove is under the stairways with a table and ornaments, sometimes flowers; rooms lead off to right and left, a beautiful house.

In the 1950s I was staying with friends in Norfolk, and one day we visited friends near the border with Suffolk. As we turned into the driveway, I recognized the house immediately: on entering the hallway, the staircases were just as I had dreamt them. It was a very strange feeling, like going home. The house was a rectory.

After this physical visit, the dream never recurred again. Had I been haunting this house during my dream state, or had I lived there in a previous life?

There have been accounts of people astral travelling to places and being recognised later on; for example, one woman had dreamt of repeatedly visiting a hotel her husband was staying in. Later, this woman decided to join her husband on holiday. When she checked in, one of the chamber maids recognised her as the 'ghost'! Some women wrote to me of visiting a place in a dream as it was centuries ago, and when they looked at themselves, they were wearing clothes in keeping with that era. People who are seen while astral travelling are often seen wearing the current fashion. I sense it's possible to be seen as a ghost or have your presence felt when visiting a particular place in an astral dream (see Chapter VII on astral projection).

Some childhood dreams involved seeing apparitions. Mr J.W. from Gloucestershire recalled that as a child he would just have gone off to sleep when he could hear a rustling noise coming down the stairs from the attic. Then, much to his alarm, an old woman in a Victorian silk dress would come over and vigorously shake him in his cot. He would then cry out for his mother who would rush into the room, all concerned, reassuring him that there wasn't anybody there. This experience stopped when he was about seven years old.

Later on, as a teenager, Mr J.W. would see people whom he later found out had died that same day. First he saw an elderly neighbour, Mr Green, on his way home from school and waved over, as he always did – unaware that Mr Green had already passed over to the other side of life. The other person was a close friend of the family. Mr J.W. had returned home from school and said 'Better put the kettle on, Mum, Tony's coming down the road on his bike'.

The Future in Your Dreams

There was a deadly silence: 'Don't say such a thing! We've just had a terrible phone call saying that Tony was killed on his bike, at the top of the road, three hours ago!'

Ms E. Ross-Fraser, from Dornoch, Scotland, recalled that when she was a child, living in London, she dreamt of a strange woman coming over to her bed and saying 'Come with me'. Ms Ross-Fraser did not wish to go with this woman, who thought that Ms Ross-Fraser was her daughter, for some reason. The noticeable thing was that this woman was wearing a very strange hat; it was cone shaped, pointed and had a pale blue veil floating from the top of it. As the woman tried to pick her up, the child shouted out for her real Mummy and her mother would come into the bedroom. The woman in the pointed hat would always have vanished by this time. Many years later, some demolition work was carried out and a dress with a pointed hat and a veil were found behind the bricks of Ms Ross-Fraser's old bedroom. As an adult, Ms Ross-Fraser also experienced premonition dreams that came true. This shows that she is naturally psychic. Finally I would like to include one of my own experiences:

> When I was a teenager we lived in a pleasant Victorian terraced house. My room was upstairs; the rooms were large and airy. We lived beside the seaside in Tynemouth. This particular week, relatives were staying with us, so I had to share a room with my sister. The room had two beds. My bed was nearest to the window; my sister's bed was next to the wall. We were sleeping this night as usual – the whole house was asleep.
>
> I woke up, and it was light like daylight. 'Ah, morning', I thought, so I opened the curtains to see what the sky was like. I loved looking out of the window to see the beautiful morning skies. But, to my shock and surprise, when I opened the curtains, it was still night time. Indigo sky with silver stars! I let the curtain fall, closed again. It was still light in the room. I turned round slowly to face the door. Beside the door was a large white figure: it was floating a few inches above ground level, and was bigger than a man. I concluded to myself that it was not a man – although of the same vague shape, it was a lot bigger. I could not make out any features. The reason for this was its brilliance, which was getting brighter and brighter, and in this brilliance was a great power. I found it difficult to look at the central part of the shape because of

its intensity. It was breathtaking. The only similarity I have seen here on earth is that of fork lightning, if you can imagine this lightning clumped together. This figure emanated light into the whole room. The light seemed to block out everything else in the room: I could no longer see my sister's bed or any furniture. I began to feel the power beaming over towards me from the door area, and was afraid. Planet earth seemed like a ping-pong ball. The power exerted was more powerful than a volcano or high mountains. I put my head under the covers and pinched my face to make sure I was awake! When I looked up again, it was still there. I sensed that the power was neither good nor bad. It was clear that it could be used to strike down or to strengthen. I couldn't ask it any questions, because I couldn't speak! But in myself I acknowledged it, and though, curiously, I was pleased to have had a visit, my thoughts were 'would it please go'! It stayed for a little while with me and then glided serenely and silently out of the room, through the slightly opened door. The room went back to normal, dark. After a few minutes of staying wide awake, I gingerly got out of bed and went into the hall. It was all reassuringly dark. I ran upstairs to my parents' room, and asked if I could stay with them! They just said yes, and didn't ask me why at the age of thirteen I wanted to sleep beside them! I told my mother about it some time later, and she said it must have been an angel. My sister had been quite unaware of it, and was surprised!

Chapter III

Winning Dreams

Have you ever wished you could dream about the numbers of the lottery and win? Well, some people have! Others have won on the horses and yet others have won in competitions. I have to say that overall only about 7 per cent of the dreams that I researched related to winning a fortune; still, it just goes to show that nothing is impossible!

Mrs D. Williams of Suffolk wrote to me of the following dream, which came true almost immediately. It was as if she woke up and knew it was going to be her lucky day! She wrote:

> I do a lot of crossword competitions in a weekly magazine, and after doing them for years yet never winning anything, I had a dream one night that I had won a basket of fruit. I told my husband about the dream the next day. Two days later I received a letter in the post, which my husband rushed to give me. As soon as I touched the envelope, before opening the letter, I said to my husband 'I bet it's that fruit basket I dreamt about the other night'. Sure enough, that's exactly what I had won. The reason it seemed so strange to me was that after years of doing competitions I should win the exact prize I dreamed of, even though there were many other prizes to be won. With the fruit basket, I'd also won a bottle of Malibu, which wasn't in my dream, but came as a nice surprise as it's my favourite drink, and I hate fruit! My husband says things like 'could I now please dream that I've won the car, or the big cash prize!'

Although most of the women who wrote to me foresaw an actual event in a dream, one or two did have symbolic dreams which they then interpreted either by looking up a dream dictionary or by pondering over the interpretation themselves. Carole Taylor from Blackpool was one such person. She wrote to me with a dream about money, not realizing that the first part of her dream was symbolic, and the rest was an actual clue as to where to find the lucky win! Her dream included a theme which involved a duvet and being temporarily deaf because of the noise of a derelict house being demolished nearby. Puzzled, Carole looked up the meanings in a dream dictionary, and found that the dream indicated some sort of financial prosperity.

In the second part of the dream, Carole's grandmother appeared telling her that if she bought a yellow bulldozer then things would change much for the better. So, that weekend Carole and her mother looked through some car boot sales for toy bulldozers – they found every colour but yellow so didn't bother. The following week, Carole went into her local newsagent to buy a lottery ticket. She noticed a little yellow bulldozer in the window which she bought. The next weekend Carole, her mother and her grandfather all won a small amount of money on the lottery at the same time. Next day, by way of celebrating, Carole bought herself a scratch card and to her amazement won a further two thousand pounds. Carole, like most of the other women, noticed that her premonition dreams were very realistic compared to other dreams. Another interesting point is that if Carole has ever mislaid something, she will often dream about where it is. It does seem that we are much more receptive to clear visions while in the dream state.

Miss S. J. Mackay of Sheffield is interested in horse racing, and wrote to me about this particular dream:

> In 1991 I had planned to back Lester Piggott's mount in the St Leger Stakes, but on the night before I dreamt Toulon would win. When I woke up I believed that the race had already been run, so I was glad to be told it hadn't, so that I could go to the bookmakers and put my money on Toulon, ridden by Pat Eddery. Toulon won! It came in first at odds of 5–2 favourite.

This reminds me of an experience I once had when I was quite young. My husband and I didn't have very much money at that time, being newly married. I switched on the radio and heard two commentators arguing that Red Rum could not possibly win for a third time, but I just knew he would. I looked out of my window at a betting shop, but I had never been in one before – anyway, what would I tell my husband when he got home if the horse lost! I decided against putting on a bet, for these reasons, and would you believe it? Yes, Red Rum won at 8–1! But then again that is the nature of a gamble. Still, it did reinforce in me a belief in my sixth sense, to trust in your own sixth sense, so that was good!

Another person to have a near miss on the horses was Eileen

Winning Dreams

Smith of Hampshire. She dreamt of a winner in the Grand National, but it was such a no-hoper that her husband didn't back it. Then the horse won! Mrs Smith did go on to win the lottery, however, dreaming of five of the correct numbers (four numbers and the bonus). Like Miss Mackay, Mrs Smith had such a vivid and realistic dream that she couldn't make out at first whether it had been a dream or not.

Most of the women found these types of dream quite helpful because they had brought them money! Another woman who was thus blessed was Mrs E. Wordsworth, from Wiltshire. She tells us of a dream she had in 1994:

> One Friday night I dreamt that I was at a party and noticed a rather plain, youngish man sitting on the floor, looking lonely, so I asked him his name and he replied 'Trigger, like the chap in "Only Fools and Horses" – in fact I'm so like him that I'm known as Double Trigger'. I went downstairs to get my breakfast and read the morning paper. In the sports report the racing correspondent suggested 'Double Trigger' in the three-thirty. I was so delighted that I told the butcher opposite, and all the people in the Post Office, that I intended to go to Lambourne's and put on my first bet ever! Of course it won and I pocketed several pounds. It has won ever since (except when he was taken to Australia and had a virus).

Mrs Wordsworth was so delighted she wrote to Double Trigger's owner about the dream too.

Lord Kilbracken, formerly John Godley, frequently dreamt of horse-race winners and would notify his friends of this. One day he notified a national newspaper of ten of his dream winners (one of which was a double!). Eight of these horses won, which pleased himself and other backers. For those who are interested, further details can be found in his book *Tell Me The Next One* (Gollanz, 1950).

Mrs Ogilvie of Falkirk, Scotland, wrote in to tell me of a similar dream which her late husband had. In this dream, Mr Ogilvie dreamt that he had won on two horses, ridden by Lester Piggott and Willie Carson, so in the morning he looked out for these jockeys' names in the morning paper, backed their horses, and won!

The late Ken Druitt, an esoteric and writer from Gloucestershire, said that there is a distinction to be made between psychic dreams (such as those described above), which relate to luck and worldly concerns, and the more spiritual dreams which I discuss in the 'Gifts in Dreams' section below. The former can be picked up in the atmosphere and the latter, 'gifts in dreams', can be received from spiritual, celestial and astral spheres.

Gifts in Dreams and Dreams of Achievement

By gifts in dreams, I also mean inspirations which lead to concrete help in some way, such as dreaming of an idea, or a plot for a book, and then that dream materialising in the real world. For example, John Langé from Dundee, Scotland, told me that when he was a teenager, he wanted to enter a 'Blue Peter' competition on TV, but didn't know what to draw. He dreamt of a picture of a swan and drew it the next morning, as soon as he woke up. He then entered it into the competition and, to his great amazement and satisfaction, won!

This brings me on to the next section on dreams of this nature. In the following dreams the dreamer receives a brain-wave idea or seems to acquire new skills previously unknown to them. Maria Dean, now a nurse in London, wrote about a dream she had as a teenager:

> Before I had this dream, I was hopeless at mathematics. I came bottom all the time, and didn't know my times tables, as I was never taught. Then I had a dream. In the dream, I was standing behind a stall at the school fete as I had to sell the things on the stall, even though I didn't want to. At first there was no one, then all of a sudden everyone at once wanted to buy something from me: for example someone said 'I want 50 of those at 50p each', and I said 'Oh that's £...' and came out with the price. I did this for others with difficult sums, and was able to tell everyone what they had to pay. All of a sudden Mum woke me up for college. I told her not to talk to me for the moment, while I rushed and got the calculator. I could remember all the sums and the prices I came up with in my dream. I couldn't believe it when the calculator told me I was right. I told my Mum and she just laughed. It all seemed like a miracle to me! This is the one which the dream master from the *Daily Mirror* could not explain.

Winning Dreams

This brings me on to a similar account as experienced by Edgar Cayce, a photographer and ex-Sunday school teacher with prophetic gifts. Cayce was not very good at school either, but he soon discovered that after falling asleep in the classroom he had mysteriously learnt all the things required for that lesson (and for others) and soon proceeded to become top of the class! People soon got to hear of Cayce's remarkable knowledge, and later asked him the solution for all sorts of things, including health problems. Cayce, although not formally trained as a doctor, was able to diagnose correctly and suggest cures for numerous illnesses.

This reminds me of similar dreams recorded in the *Hasedra Reigenki* (a fifteenth-century Japanese record). One account tells of a priest who could not memorise a difficult part of scripture while awake, yet in his dream he learnt it all in one night and could still remember it when he woke up! Another man, having observed religious rules of abstinence and then going along to a temple for a certain incubation time (seven, twenty-one or one hundred days was the choice), dreamt that he had been healed following a visit from a young boy telling him this. In the morning the man woke up and found himself healed of a previously incurable skin disease. There are many such accounts of healings given in the *Hasedra Reigenki*.

I would like to include a contemporary event about someone who wants to be known as A.B.L. When she was seventeen, she was contemplating which path she should take in life. A minister friend of the family said that he would pray for God to give A.B.L. a gift, and show her which path to take in life. She went to bed pondering this. In the morning, A.B.L. woke up and looked ecstatic, saying she had dreamt that she could sculpt the most beautiful figures, and she proceeded to draw the numerous sketches which she had dreamt about. That day A.B.L. bought some clay and created the most breathtaking works of art – even though she had never sculpted in her life before! After one look at her work, she was offered an unconditional place at Stafford Art College, which was quite an achievement as there were only a few students taken on each year, and only two colleges in the whole country that taught representational art! When she went to Amsterdam for a holiday she noticed that one of her sculptures was identical to a famous bust, even though she had not been there before; was she perhaps channelling this, or did the idea come from a previous lifetime, or

The Future in Your Dreams

was it just coincidence? One could be sceptical and say that she may have seen it in a book, but I was there at the time all this was happening and can say that it was not imitated, it just seemed like a pure coincidence! Her sculptures can be seen on the Internet today.

In fact, many artists and writers say that dreams have played an important part in their work. For example, some of Salvador Dali's best-known paintings were inspired by his dreams. Mary Shelley's novel *Frankenstein* was dreamt of before she wrote it. Following a conversation with friends one night, about the possibility of scientists creating life in the future, she went to bed and dreamt up the scenario; this, coupled with the perfect backdrop, the east coast of Scotland, ended up becoming the popular story *Frankenstein*. The British poet Samuel Taylor Coleridge said that he was inspired to write a poem, the 'Kubla Khan', as he had dreamt up the lines and found them intriguing. Many modern writers (such as Agatha Christie) have been assisted in dreams when thinking up plots and storylines for their novels, and others such as J. B. Priestley say that some books seem effortless to write, as though they were receiving some divine assistance. Robert Louis Stevenson tells of how complete stories came to him in dreams. In his book *Across the Plains* Graham Greene told one of his audiences that he would dream up the storylines for many of his books at night, and if he had been puzzled about anything in his work, he would have a good night's sleep and the problem would be solved by morning. I know it sounds like a cliché because so many people do say 'sleep on it' if they have a decision to make, but they tend to say this because it's true!

When the poet Dante Alighieri died in 1321, there were thirteen cantos missing from his epic poem the *Divine Comedy*. One night, one of Dante's sons had a remarkable dream. He dreamt that the missing section of 'Paradiso' was to be found in an old alcove, which had been covered up by a mat, in an old house where they had once lived. On awakening, Dante's son went to explain all of this to the current owner of the old house. Fortunately, the new owner had not disturbed the cantos and they were still hidden there! This is why we have the complete version of Dante's *Divine Comedy* now. Brilliant!

A famous dream by King Solomon, renowned for his wisdom, wealth and love of life, is recorded in 1 Kings, ch. 3 v. 5 and onwards. Solomon had a dream one night in which God asked him what he would like. Solomon replied:

> 'Eternal God, you have made me King instead of my father David and I am a mere child, I know not how to go about my business. I, your servant, am surrounded by your chosen people, too great to be numbered. So grant me an understanding mind to govern your people and that I may distinguish between right and wrong. For who can bear the weight of this government?'
>
> God replied: 'Because you have asked neither for a long life for yourself nor for the death of your enemies, but for insight and justice, I now do as you have asked. I hereby give you a wise, thoughtful mind, so that never afterwards shall your equal rise, as never has your equal lived. Also I give you what you did not ask for: both wealth and honour, so that no king shall ever be your equal. And if you live my life keeping my rules and orders, as did your father, I will give you a long life.'
>
> Then Solomon woke and, although it was a dream, it soon became a reality as the dream was accomplished.

Some of the other dreams might seem insignificant when compared to Solomon's dream, but then again he was the king, and it seems that people get dreams about what is concerning them the most.

The twelfth-century nun Hildegard of Bingen started composing religious songs on topics such as divine love and vision, following an inspirational dream at the age of forty. Many famous musicians such as Bach and Beethoven believed they were tapping into another realm and bringing music down from God.

And one last example: Napoleon was reported to have used his dreams to plan military campaigns, with great success. He would write down his dreams on awakening and then try out the plans as if playing a game of chess.

It seems that in our sleep we are able to access information not normally available while awake, such as the sifting through of ideas in one's unconscious mind. Esoteric groups believe that some psychic people have access to a book called the Akashic records (Sanskrit) where all knowledge is stored concerning the past, present and future, and that one can gain access to this information through one's dreams in the astral planes or while in a relaxed or meditative state. The Akashic records have also been described as a type of celestial memory bank, and also as the Book of Life.

Carl Jung believed that members of all races have access to a pool of knowledge and wisdom, which he called the collective unconscious. According to Jung the collective unconscious includes thought patterns called archetypes, which have developed through the centuries. Jung thought that these archetypes have enabled people to react to certain situations in a similar way to their ancestors. He also believed in the idea of synchronisation, where two unrelated people could invent the same thing even though living miles apart. A good example is that of Thomas Edison (an American inventor) and Joseph Swan (a British chemist): both men invented the electric light bulb at around the same time. Were they tapping into some communal think-tank? Or was it just a happy coincidence? There are lots of uncanny synchronisations just like this one.

Jung's studies of mythology convinced him that archetypal figures of God and supernatural powers are deeply rooted in the collective unconscious. Jung believed that religion played a major role in human life by enabling people to express an unconscious need for religious experience. Jungians believe that there is a bank of mythological ideas and icons (images) which can be inherited in the memory and hence tend to crop up in dream land; for example, a father can be seen by the child as a hero who then appears as a superman or an ogre in a symbolic dream.

Symbolic Dreams

There are examples of symbolic dreams dotted around in this book. I would like to include a couple of examples here, first from someone who doesn't wish to be named:

> I was about to get married. Secretly, I felt pushed into it, by my family and the wedding guests' expectations. Then I had this dream two weeks before the wedding. I was standing at the top of a steep road; there were houses on either side. I walked a short way down and went into a shop; my wedding dress had arrived and I opened the long white box excitedly, pulling away the white tissue paper. I was shocked to see that the whole dress, and the veil and the shoes,

were in black! It was a beautifully made dress, the one I had chosen, so I put it on; I was wearing the black shoes, which were made of fine leather and were pointed at the toes. When I got out of the shop I ran for a bus which was across the road. I got in, and the bus pulled off in a hurry, just as I had got into it. I sat down feeling quite alarmed. Just then, the brakes on the bus gave way and the bus careered down the road at great speed. The driver just about managed to steer the bus round the corner at the bottom of the road. The sea was in sight from the side of the bus. We all got off the bus; I had to struggle back up the hill, holding my big black wedding dress, which was such a heavy weight. I eventually got back to the top of the road after much sweat and toil.

This was a symbolic warning of 'marry in haste, repent at leisure'; the dreamer did eventually get back to where she started, but after how much hassle, and after how long? Even if it is just two weeks before the wedding, if you're not sure, and you get this type of dream . . . don't do it! One can actually go to marriage guidance before getting married!

Another dream involved a woman who dreamt that she was trying on her wedding outfit. It was all perfect, apart from the black veil. Soon after, this woman's fiancé was diagnosed with a degenerative illness, which had no cure. The woman decided to go ahead with the wedding and committed herself to looking after her husband as his main carer.

Symbolic dreams about the future are usually quite straightforward. It could be said that the first case above showed a dream coming from the dreamer's own mind, a churning-over of ongoing current events. Nevertheless, the message was still there.

Mrs D. Paterson of Aberdeen wrote to me of an experience she had. She was finishing a typing class when she felt inspired to write some poems for her newly born grandchild. She was amazed because prior to this she had longed to write but could not get two lines to rhyme! When she got home she wrote down some of the poems which came into her head, and has written several poems that many people have enjoyed reading. This sometimes happens when we least expect it: say, while ironing or washing the dishes and thinking of nothing in particular we might have a 'hunch' about something or get a telepathic message, gain an insight into something or get inspiration to write some poetry. It is probably due to our stress-free state at the time! All the creative arts are closely linked with having psychic abilities and what is known as the Alpha state of thinking. The Alpha state is a light trance state where the electrical activity of the brain has slowed down. We go into this state when we daydream. It is possible to become more tuned into our creativity and we may have a sense of being connected to the universal unconscious mind during this time.

There are several stories of writers accurately writing about a future event (making a prediction) in a fictional novel. I have done this too – strange but true!

Chapter IV

Previews of the Future

The Gate of Horn

The Ancient Greeks believed that there were two gates that led to dreams: the Gate of Ivory for everyday dreams, and the Gate of Horn for dreams that come true.

Many women who answered my questionnaires said they were amazed when they first realised that their dreams were coming true. Some said they felt shocked or afraid by the experience, but have since come to terms with it. I once had the same feelings of 'what's going on?'; I felt amazement, disbelief and apprehension all at the same time! Then, at the risk of being thought of as mad or at least a bit unusual, I decided to tell my mother about it. I just felt she might be able to help. She didn't look overly surprised at what I told her, and said with confidence: 'Just think of yourself as having a special gift. That's good if you have dreams about the future. You might as well accept it rather than feeling it's alien, because having that attitude is just going to make you feel unnecessarily worried. It's a perfectly natural experience for some people.' It transpired that other members of my family had been likewise gifted, so it came as no surprise to my Mum, but she looked a little sad because of course she knew that I would be in the minority in talking about this ability, and that it would be none too wise to go broadcasting it. People tend to fall into two camps: the believers (because they too have experienced it) and the sceptics who say 'Ridiculous!' and 'Now, back in the real world!'

I tried for quite some time to find like-minded people but to no avail, so I consoled myself by writing my precognitive dreams in a dream book. I always dated it and left the opposite page blank to record the actual event. Sometimes the dream came true after three days, others took weeks or even months. I kept a dream diary to see if there were any common links, for example events or times when my precognitive dreams were most abundant; I can't say that they did occur more frequently in any particular month, but I can say that some geographical areas seem to be much more conducive to premonition dreams than others. There is no conclusive map as further research needs to be done in this area.

Preview dreams fell into two areas: (1) previews of personal events such as dreaming of buildings, places and foreseeing future experiences; (2) previews of news events or world affairs. I call them previews, as opposed to warning dreams, because the recipients were unable to alter the outcome of these dreams. Some of the dreams concerned previews of places that would be visited later, and I would like to commence with these.

Miss M. Bristow had several such dreams. She recalls:

> I dreamt I was on a school outing to a stately home. My school friends and I were running from room to room, and I ran to a window and looked out on to a beautiful formal garden. Many years later, long after I'd left school, my church went on an outing to Penhurst Palace in Kent. I went into one of the rooms and recognised it as the room from my dream. It had a large window at one end and I knew exactly what I was going to see out of it. Sure enough, when I looked out of the window there was a formal garden, exactly as in the dream. I had never been to Penhurst Palace before.

This reminds me of similar dreams that I have had about mansion houses and stately homes. But I would like to start at the beginning, because the first house I dreamt about turned out to be a very remarkable place indeed.

I was in Spain, at my parents' house, feeling in a state of turmoil with the prospect of returning to Scotland with no house and no furniture! I had given it all up, thinking I was going to stay in Spain for a year – but then I decided to return to University and finish my degree, instead of taking a year out. Cezar (my Dad's Spanish friend) said 'Trust in God', so I did, because from that distance I felt pretty stranded! Following this, for two nights running I had a strange dream.

In the dream I found myself walking along a coastline: it was dark, wet and windy. As I walked along, dawn broke, and I could see large houses and streets from the beach. I recognised it to be Broughty Ferry, and I wondered if this was where I was to get a house as I had a friend who lived there, but in the dream I was told that my friend no longer lived there and that I should walk further along the coast. I became aware that in my shorts, tee-shirt and sandals I was inappropriately dressed for the Scottish climate and

I saw that it would soon be daylight, so I hurried along the beach away from Broughty Ferry heading north until I came to the next seaside area. Feeling totally bewildered, I turned left and went through a tunnel.

Daybreak came and a man passed me in the tunnel. He lifted his hat to me and said 'Morning'. I became aware that I was in a dream. 'I must go back to Spain', I thought, but, feeling led, I proceeded up a straight and narrow road and went on towards the main street. On my right I noticed a large pale building with lots of red ivy climbing up it. I carried on up the road and turned into a row of Victorian houses. The sun was coming out and I still had on all my Spanish holiday clothes – shorts and tee-shirt. Anyway, I felt in a lighter mood and then I heard a familiar voice shout 'Hey Annabelle!'. I turned around and it was a friend of mine whom I had put up once when he was in between houses. 'What are you doing here? I thought you were in Spain. Want to come in for a cup of tea?' I agreed to stay for a short time.

The house had a spacious hall and a few rooms leading off. I proceeded to climb up the stairs, noticing the red carpet with little white flowers and that the house was quite old fashioned, pre-war in its decor. I went into a room upstairs and saw a large woman with long untidy hair, a 'salt of the earth' type person wearing a crocheted shawl. She had three grown-up daughters and several cats. My friend Rod introduced us and then said 'I have to go now. You can stay here if you like because they'll rent this place out to you for the University season, no problem, OK?' and then off he went. I wanted to go too, because I thought this was all very strange. How did Rod know these people? They weren't like his usual friends. Yet I felt very protected in this room. Sunlight came through my window and I woke up, back in my parents' house in Spain. Straight away, I felt a little less anxious about my accommodation worries!

The next night I went straight back into the dream, and I was with the woman from the previous night. Again I felt quite at home, and felt that I could really be myself because no one was judging me or expecting anything from me, so I could just have a relaxing time. I had a look around the house. It was a lovely house, and it had a nice walled garden. The house had a lot of character, which I liked. I made an arrangement with the ladies to stay there when I got back from Spain, so everyone was happy.

On my return to Scotland I stayed with my sister Elizabeth. She saw an advert in the paper for a house to let and I phoned up about it. We went to look at it, but three-quarters of the way there I said, 'Oh, let's turn back, it's too far away from the University'. But Elizabeth said, 'Might as well go and look at it now, we're nearly there'. I had my doubts, but when I saw the place I was glad that I had gone along with her.

Needless to say, I moved into the house of my dreams – literally! When I got inside the house, I immediately recognised the stair carpet (red with little white flowers) and the pre-war style rooms; then, as I was walking down the stairs, the owner said 'I don't normally say this, because others want to see it, but would you like the house?' I said, yes, I would! So I got the keys the next day. The old lady said she liked the look of me and my presence for some reason, but she didn't know why! She and her friend were not at all like the women in my dream, and neither was my friend Rod familiar with the house. I find all of this a mystery, yet the house and its location were accurate. Were the people in my dream the inhabitants of the house generally (ghosts) or were they perhaps the owner's guides? I would more or less say that they fell into the first category. I was given the house 'for the season' (their words) and I am very grateful to the woman for offering it to me!

Once I was settled into the house, I went for a walk along the beach. On my return, out of curiosity, I decided to walk through one of several tunnels leading off from the beach, and when I looked to my right I saw a large house with red ivy growing up the wall, just as it had been in my dream. Amazing!

Intriguingly, while in that Victorian house in particular I had so many dreams about the future. This led me to believe that some houses or areas are much more conducive to premonition dreaming than others. I have certainly found this to be the case, personally. I was living in Carnoustie, in Angus, Scotland, quite happily; I had lots of friends and everything was going well at University. My sister lived in the area, so I had no particular plans of moving to England in the near future. Yet I started dreaming, having previews of moving to the South of England, meeting people who felt like soulmates in my dreams, people who made me feel happy. I recognised them when I was dreaming, I seemed to have known them all my life in the dreams, but did not know who they were when I woke up! This sort of double life puzzled me, but also fascinated me.

In one of a series of dreams I was in the South of England and in a magnificent house, Dodington. Wearing a long blue ballgown, I walked down a grand double staircase swirling into a single staircase with banisters on both sides; this led to a spacious main hall. I then turned, and went through a huge door which was slightly ajar, and I found myself in a spectacular ballroom with mirrors and large windows looking out on to a garden. In the garden was a square bird bath, and beyond that a lake and woods. The garden had one tree in it, which a gardener was concerned about. I turned around and went back into the hall, which had huge white double pillars with beautiful high arches; this arch shape was reflected in the arched alcove on the stair landing and the arched window above, shedding light into the house. The rest of the decor had a most pleasant colour scheme of blue and white. The servants' quarters had a plain narrow staircase and a red carpet.

Then I went into a dining room, which was very large. It had an oblong mahogany table with a grandfather clock behind it. An older man with a white moustache was sitting there, wearing a smoking jacket. Clearly he was my host; he seemed powerful, in an archetypal way. He had the most beautiful, sparkling blue eyes; this man also had a great depth of knowledge and I felt quite captivated by him. It was as if he knew me very well, and I knew him. In a strange way, I felt as though I had come home. I couldn't put my finger on who he was and he didn't use his name. The feeling I had in the dream was that he was the then owner of Dodington. I know it sounds strange, but the truth is that I later recognised this person in this life (the expression in the eyes and his manner). It lay in my future which was still to come. He lived in the South-West of England, not in Dodington, in this life, but in an old farm house-house near Stroud in rural Gloucestershire. I believe, like many women who wrote to me of similar experiences, that it was a simple case of an action replay of a past life: in short, a reincarnation dream.

Going back now into the dream: I wanted to stay. I was just about to pull a chair over and sit down to spend some time with my companion, when one of the maids came in; she whispered to me, most urgently, not to stay there for too long, as the clock behind this gentleman was a time machine and that this man would want me to stay there forever, if he had his way. I felt she was being a spoilsport, but at the same time I felt a bit apprehensive at the prospect of not being able to leave and perhaps being captured in time! The maid's manner and pushy attitude made me become increasingly aware that I was in a dream. I had only just arrived here, in the dining room, but something in me decided to follow her advice. I hurriedly followed her in secret, along to the servants' much narrower and plainer staircase, and soon found myself outside. To my surprise, there was a car waiting there for me. I filled up the tank from a little petrol pump at the back of the house. I thought this was strange as the house seemed to belong to a previous era. Once in the car, I headed away from the house along a long drive. There was a small lodge at the end of the drive; I got out of the car and went in briefly to have a look around. It was smaller, but still elegant, round in shape and also decorated in blue and white.

After this I dreamt of two other stately homes which I instantly recognised when I moved to the South-West of England in the following year. Once again I was dressed in long, heavy and expensive gowns, in darker colours this time: a gold fitted jacket and a checked brown skirt. I was also wearing a stiff bonnet of matching colours. I was quite a young lady in the dream.

One night, I visited what I now know to be Goldney Hall in Bristol. I dreamt that my daughter was staying there and she did, later, in real life (though I saw it first in dream life). Part of Goldney Hall – the modern part – is now a hall of residence and she stayed there during the summer. The part I dreamt of was the old part, the old house and the old tower. The other place I visited in my dream was Owlpen Manor, not far from where I eventually stayed when I moved to Dursley. In my dream I went there to visit an old bedridden lady; she was in a four-poster bed, waiting for the doctor to arrive. In the present timescale I went to the very same house for afternoon tea with a friend. When I entered the old bedroom I instantly recognised it, and rushed over to look out of the window in order to confirm the rest of the dream to myself; then, viewing the old surrounding wall and layout, I had my confirmation. I had now visited the three grand houses in real life, so I knew that my destiny at this time was to be here, in the South-West of England, and no longer in Scotland.

The house mentioned in detail above was Dodington House, which is not open to the public. However, my friend Don got the job of rewiring it when he moved up from London – he was a very good electrician, having also studied to be an engineer. One day, I went to collect him in the car. The owner at the time, Guy, said I was welcome to have a look around, even though I had never met him. Needless to say, Dodington House was identical to the house in my dream, and I described all the rooms to Don before entering them. Yes, the house even had the small petrol pump outside, and the lodge, at the end of the long drive on the way out, was still painted in blue and white, as in the dream. I knew this because my colleague Marcella and her partner lived there!

Dodington House was empty and being decorated when I saw it in real life, yet the house was beautifully furnished in my dream, as mentioned. I was standing outside, chatting to the electricians, watching the most beautiful blue dragonfly I have ever seen, when I told Don and some of his mates, enthusiastically, that the house was the very same one as in my dream. 'However,' I joked, 'the colour of the decor was very different, a distinct blue and white, so obviously that wasn't quite right!' Just then someone retrieved an old postcard from a box by the nearby skip; he held it out and said, excitedly, 'Was it like this?' To my shock, it was. It was the hall of Dodington as it had once appeared in the past, with the splendid blue walls, ceiling decorations and double white pillars. All the features which I had been so impressed with in my dream were there! Fabulous! Fantastic!

The question still remained: why would I visit a place like this (in my dream), set back in time, dressed in a blue ballgown, fitted at the waist? And then visit it again in this century, in real life, dressed in modern clothes? Strange! I am quite tempted to find out a bit more about the history of these old places which I dreamt about. Maybe one day!

Eastern scientists are more at home with the idea of reincarnation (also known as the transmigration of souls) than Western scientists. Nevertheless, recall of past lives is common to both Eastern and Western civilisations. Sai Baba of Puttaparti, born in Southern India in 1926, claimed to be a reincarnation of Sai Baba of Shirdi (West India), who had died eight years earlier. This soul would have been resting between lives. Until the age of fourteen Sai Baba had been a normal boy, but then he started having recollections of his past life, in dreams and visions, and began reciting long passages of Vedantic philosophy. Later on he was noted for gathering devotees around him and performing miracles.

The author Taylor Caldwell wrote a book called *The Romance of*

Atlantis. This was based on her dream recollections of a past life at a time when Atlantis was about to become a lost city. She wrote a novel at the age of twelve, which included details of people's clothes and a description of one of her romances, saying that she was a princess in that life time. In around 350 BC Plato made reference to Atlantis, having heard about it from Egyptian stories. Plato called it an enchanted kingdom, with the most advanced civilisation on Earth. According to legend, the Atlanteans used various crystals to bring about premonition dreams; they also used crystals to promote flying dreams!

Edgar Cayce made a prediction that the tip of Atlantis would be found somewhere around the Bahamian island of Bimini, in 1968 and 1969. In 1968 a fishing guide found a pattern of stones under the water near Bimini; archaeologists followed this up and found chunks of marble pillars submerged alongside an old road underneath the sea. Cayce made many prophecies about Atlantis; one was that reincarnated Atlanteans would be drawn to rebuild the emerging land. Cayce's son, Hugh Lynn, once said that his father 'didn't like to make predictions. He believed in free will, and didn't like to influence people who might be susceptible to suggestion'.*
I would agree with that sentiment.

I would like to include one more of my own dreams in this section. I've noticed that I always get a premonition dream when I'm needing a bit of support. When I had this dream, I found myself at a big crossroads in my life and was considering what to do, trying to have some vision for the future. I was acknowledging the fact that I was not being true to myself at that time and was on the brink of setting myself free from a tight situation.

That night I dreamt that I journeyed far south again, somewhere in England. I was walking down a road, and the sun was shining. I approached a house, and an old lady was standing there. She welcomed me in and showed me into a downstairs room, on the right of a corridor. Inside this room there was a long dark wooden table surrounded by very high-backed elaborate dining chairs. The room was filled with green houseplants and a grey parrot was sitting by the window in a large ornate silver cage. The old lady spoke to me, and I noticed she had lovely long plaited hair, double-wrapped across the top of her head in the form of a band

---

* In *Predictions*, ed. J. Fisher and P. Commins; Sidgwick and Jackson, 1981, p. 84.

(two plaits meeting). I remember thinking 'what a lovely hairstyle'. She told me that if I had any problems or difficulties at all, she was willing and able to help me. I talked to her for a while and she gave me lots of very good advice, then I left.

In the morning I told my daughter about the dream. The old lady had given me some useful advice, and although I couldn't remember what it was I was left with the impression that somebody wanted to help and I felt greatly relieved. In March that year, we went to Bath for a holiday and booked into a recommended guest house. I said to myself: 'I wonder if that lady will be here?' But I was soon to discover that the lady in my dream was not there. The holiday came and went. I put the dream to the back of my mind, although at the time I recognised it as being a premonition dream, so I was expecting it 100 per cent to come true.

Later that year I was booked in for a short course on Religious Studies in London. On my last night I was supposed to go out with the rest of the group, to the Hare Krishna Temple, but decided not to, because I had already visited that particular temple before on my own. So I just told everybody not to expect me because of this, and also because I was going to have an early night. At around 5 p.m. I was sitting on my bed in the hotel room, feeling bored. I started to look through a magazine and came across a section advertising fortune-tellers. I thought, 'Oh, you never know, they might be quite good in London', so I phoned up a few. I couldn't believe it! Either they were booked up for the next fortnight, or they charged extortionate prices, or I had to leave messages on answering machines, so after several attempts I thought, 'right, this is the last one'. A lady answered the phone; she sounded young and friendly, and she said that I could go and see her right away! I was a bit taken aback but thought, 'why not?' So I took down the instructions on how to get there.

It was a Sunday evening and it was 6 p.m. I made my way to the tube station but was sure I would get lost because I had to make several connections. I met a girl in the Underground station and asked her if this was the right train to the area I was heading for. She said it was and that she was going there too, so I travelled with her. She lived in the street which ran parallel to Mrs Alexander's house. 'Fancy! What a coincidence!' I said. I felt pleased, even elated, at the ease of my journey and at having met my friendly and helpful guide. When I got there, I noticed an old

The Future in Your Dreams

lady looking out of a room upstairs. Yes, it was her, the old lady from my dream! I recognised her straight away, as she wore her hair in a plait on the top of her head just as in the dream. She told me that she normally spoke to people in the room upstairs, but would I like to follow her into the downstairs room (on the right of the corridor) today . . . and there it was, exactly the same room as in my dream, with the parrot, plants, ornate chairs – everything! So I decided to pay particular attention to what she advised me.

I told the lady, who was called Joy, about my dream, and she was so pleased that a meeting had been 'arranged'. She didn't seem to be surprised – although I was, big time! She didn't use a crystal ball or anything, but she told me so many things: that I would have a pretty tough time at first, but that out of seemingly nothing would come much, and that I was to take opportunities at once because thinking about things at a later date was never much good, sometimes it can take ten years for the same type of opportunity to present itself again. She also accurately predicted improvements in my future which have since come true: I started to work towards my own progress and self-development. Sadly, Mrs Alexander, who was a good age, has since died. I was amazed and delighted to meet this lady, and I am pleased to know that there are people who use their abilities so unselfishly to help others.

The imagination can be a great enhancement to premonition dreams and this helps us to recall distinguishing features on awakening. Samantha Jane Carr wrote to me of a dream she had when she was fourteen, about the nineteenth-century mystic and writer, Emily Brontë:

> My Mum, Dad, and family used to go on a holiday every year. Once, before going on holiday, I had a dream about one of the Brontë sisters, Emily. I was on the beach and I was having a chat to her. I told her that we were going on holiday for a week to Yorkshire soon, and that we would be visiting the Brontë Parsonage. Then all of a sudden she turned into a cast iron statue, and all this classical music was playing from nowhere. Then I heard a voice calling 'Emily, Emily!' The next day, I told my brother about my dream. I had heard of the Brontë sisters, but didn't know that there was one called Emily. While we were on holiday in Yorkshire, we visited the Brontë

Parsonage and there was the cast iron statue of the three Brontë sisters. I was so scared. I felt goose-bumps all over. I told my brother 'there's that statue'. Just then we heard some background music coming from the house, which was as in my dream. I'd never been to the Brontë Parsonage in my life and we have not studied the Brontës at school so how did I know so much about the statue and that one of the sisters was called Emily?

Sometimes a real-life event will trigger something from a premonition dream and the person is then able to recall the dream in some detail. This happened to Mrs L. Rogers of Surrey. She had a dream about a college she had never been to. Her brother was there, but more unusually her aunt and uncle were also in the dream, although she didn't see much of them ordinarily. Some time later, they were all at the college for her brother's graduation; the gathering was just as in the dream and this triggered what you might call an action-replay. Mrs Rogers was able to recognise the layout of the college room.

Mrs D. Woolford from Stevenage had a dream of a road as it had been several years in the past. The strange thing was that her daughter had just bought a house there:

> In my dream I saw a row of houses, with a stretch of grass in front; opposite this ran a small path with a row of trees on either side. Shortly after this, we went to see my daughter's new house. Except for the railway line opposite, it was as I had seen it in my dream and I felt I had been there before. While we were waiting outside for my daughter and her family I had a chat with her neighbour, and found out that several years ago there had been some trees and a small path where the railway line was now!

Mrs Woolford was rather taken aback by this and told her husband and family.

It seems that time, past, present and future, can all be accessed in the dream state. This dream was a review, as well as a preview, which is possible in Universal time. According to recent research by Dr Michael Newton, some of his patients were quite able to do this (i.e. remember the long distant past) under hypnosis, with interesting results.

Dreams About the Future

Jillian Hunter wrote to me of her premonition dream concerning a job:

> Some years ago I dreamt that I was invited to an interview at John Smith's Brewery. This was to be held at 2 p.m. in Halifax. Approximately two years later, I saw a job advertised in the job centre. When I enquired about it, I was told that the position was at John Smith's Brewery. I applied and got asked to an interview. The interview was at 2 p.m. I remembered the dream and was convinced that I would get the job – I did! The job was in Barnsley, but I was later transferred to an office in Halifax!

Mr G.A., a bank manager working in Cheltenham, told me that he often dreamt of visiting his old school. Here, he would help struggling students to understand mathematics and would leave once they'd realised how to get their sums right. These were always flying dreams.

> I would fly around school, watching over students, encouraging them in sports, teaching in maths and generally protecting from bullies, etc. A particularly visual element was the flying over the fields, and my ability to do this at my old school. I've not had this dream for a while, it occurred mostly in my 20s and early 30s.

Many people seem to do spiritual work while in the dream state – thus helping to improve things in daily life.

Mrs Bristow of Surrey had a preview concerning her school – it must have been a great old school!

> I dreamt I was in my old junior school, running through the corridors. Suddenly I came across a corridor I didn't recognise. I went down it and at the end it opened out. Before me was a panoramic view, as if I was standing on a hillside looking out over a valley at the lights of a village over the hill, although I was still standing in the corridor. Some time later, some children invited me to the local school fair. I thought it would be fun to see the old school again so I went. The kids gave me a guided tour, first down the old corridor, then down a new one. This was a part of the new extension to the

school which had been built long after I left. At the end of the corridor, it opened out into a wider space and on the opposite wall was a huge mural which the children had painted – of a village on a hillside with all the houses lit up!

Our imagination can sometimes elaborate upon a dream and create variations which may seem plausible during the dream. The idea of lucid dreaming suggests that a person is aware that they are in a dream and are able to alter their dreams at will. This is not an uncommon phenomenon, and Salvador Dali was one of the more famous people with this ability. However, I do not want people to jump to the conclusion that the dream is all about the imagination and therefore a purely mental activity, because as seen in Chapter VI it is likely that the personality, memory and imagination are all faculties which also lie outside of the brain. They are endowments of spirit and continue to exist after life. The brain is an organ and like other organs it has specific functions; some of these are the categorising of information, the ability to learn a new language by connecting symbols to words, the ability to transform thoughts into words, and so on, but the actual spirit of a person, I believe, lives inside the human body and can make nocturnal journeys independent of the physical body. It has a similar appearance to the physical body, but is ethereal. It is a more ideal form, and it feels perfectly natural because it's the real you! It can also travel at great speeds.

Research has shown that premonition experiences occur more often when we are in a relaxed state, and this is why the dream state is such a good vehicle for premonitions. However, a lot of people said that they had precognitive experiences while still awake and during the hypnogogic stage, prior to dropping off to sleep.

Sometimes if I haven't seen a person for a long time I will see a clear picture of them in my mind's eye. I will then know (from experience) that the next day I will see that person. Once, my cat had gone missing for several days and then, while lying on my bed at night, a vision of my cat came into my mind. I felt reassured that he wasn't lost, and of course, there he was sitting on my doorstep in the morning! Some girls (aged fifteen to twenty-three years) wrote to me of a similar experience where they dreamt of letters arriving in the post. Hayley S. from Combs wrote:

I had this dream that I had some photos coming through the post, and thought nothing of it. The next morning I had some photos arrive through the post. This is what my dreams are normally like. I dream that something is coming and the next morning it is there.

Another lady told me about a dream of receiving a special gift which later came true. Annabel Hollis from Stroud, Gloucestershire, said:

I dreamt I received a gift of amber stones in a purse. The dream was very vivid and had a powerful impact. I woke up feeling that the dream had touched my heart in a loving way. A month later I received an amber bracelet as a Christmas present from a close friend who has since died, so this gift meant a lot to me.

News Events

David Mandell, an artist and retired lecturer (also fellow dreamer!), sometimes appears on TV and in the newspapers. He is well known for having had premonition dreams about world affairs such as the crashing of Concorde and the fall of the twin towers at the World Trade Centre in New York. Mr Mandell quickly painted, or drew, what he had seen in his dream. In the dream about the twin towers collapsing he has also shown the Statue of Liberty, in order to identify where these twin towers might be. The way in which Mr Mandell's predictions were corroborated was ingenious! He would go down to the bank and stand in front of the time and date display in that bank. Then he would ask one of the bank tellers to take a photo. The date captured above the painting of the twin towers falling was 11 September 1996. The twin towers fell, in our timescale, on 11 September 2001. In this way, no one could dispute that one of his prophetic dreams had indeed come true, as indeed many others.

Most of us do tell close friends and family, as the people who wrote to me did. The reason we need to tell people is because of the importance of the dream and the emotions that go along with it. I have become aware in the dream that somebody 'up there', a higher power, does think that these events are of crucial importance, and we the dreamers know that this information needs to be transmitted in order to avoid the problem found in the dream becoming a reality.

There is a central premonitions registry on the Internet which was set up to receive precognitive dreams. The aim was to prevent such disasters as the fall of the twin towers from happening again. The Society for Psychical Research has a website for people interested in this subject. The address is: www.spr.ac.uk.

A lot of people wrote to me about previews of national or world-wide affairs, as well as previews of news announcements. Generally, precognitive dreams of world events are not carbon copies of the actual event, but are usually close enough to rule out wishful thinking or whatever. The famous dreamer John William Dunne used to dream a lot about newspaper headlines (among other premonition dreams). In one of his news event dreams he forecast a volcanic eruption, headlined '4000 DEAD'. He could not pinpoint the exact location, but knew the approximate area. The real headline concerning the volcanic eruption, when it happened, said '40,000 DEAD', so it could be that premonition dreams give an indication of future trends, but can be interpreted with a margin of error – 'now we see but through a glass darkly' (1 Corinthians, ch. 13 v. 12).

In my experience dreams will indicate the people involved in a scene and give a description of locations, but they do not always indicate the exact time of an event. This could be because the notion of time differs between the eternal infinite state and the temporal finite state. It is possible that there is a type of cosmic Internet where all thoughts and events of this world are linked up, and which some of us can tune into: each action, thought and idea, past, present and future, is recorded on the ether. This ether is otherwise known as the collective unconscious (Carl Jung), the book of remembrance (The Bible), the Akashic records (Cayce), the astral plane (Esoterics) or the fifth dimension (Einstein). This would explain other phenomena such as synchronisation (brain-wave ideas and inventions, happening at the same time, through like-minded talented people, in different parts of the globe). The theory also covers reports of people seeing Roman soldiers charging down the street in modern times, when encountering a 'time slip', and reports of telepathy. So it seems that it is in our best interest, both as individuals and collectively, to think positively.

There have been two interesting findings on this subject. One is that people who watch the news tend to feel depressed for a few days following this. The other is that sick people who are prayed for recover more quickly than those who receive no prayer for health. Even when times are hard it's good to have faith and hope for the future.

In 1995, the BBC news reporter Martyn Lewis felt that TV producers were failing to report enough good news and therefore weren't reflecting the true world-wide situation. He enjoyed a lot of public support because this opinion resonated with many others who watched the news programmes. The BBC in defence argued that they didn't want to appear to trivialise the news.

Later, Dr Wendy Johnston and Professor Graham Davey of the University of Sussex carried out an experiment to see if negative news bulletins did tend to make people feel depressed. In their experiment, they chose three groups of people: the first group watched positive news reports, the second neutral, and the third watched negative reports. The psychological findings of these experiments showed that all three groups started off in a good frame of mind; however, those who watched the negative news reports soon became sad and anxious. These feelings then carried over into their own lives. It was advised that some good news be included in news bulletins, along with offering possible solutions to the problems given (*The British Journal of Psychology*, 1997).

A Dream Within a Dream

Quite often dreams of waking up within a dream are a sign that one is in the lucid dream state. This next dream involves an account of a plane crash. Sceptics would say that there is always the possibility of coincidence when dreaming of common events like a plane crash, but sometimes the details are specific enough to discount this theory. Mrs Welch from London dreamt she had a dream about an air crash:

> In my dream I 'awoke' in the morning; the sun was rising and shining on my bed. To my surprise, there were two airmen, in their red clothes – one was lying full length, the other one was staggering around in a daze, then fell. This all cleared and I heard the sound of planes roaring up. There was a squadron of them and they rose

up with the red/blue/white plumes of exhaust behind. They then formed a diamond pattern and were ready to form the 'bomb-burst', when the two front planes' wing tips touched and they fell to the earth in a spiral of blue and red smoke.

In a couple of days, it was announced on the news that two of the 'Red Arrows' had crashed and that the pilots were killed.

Mrs J. E. K. Kelly has experienced many different premonition dreams. This one is about an aeroplane:

I dreamt a plane crash-landed at a local airport and the plane was an Air Tours. Everything was so plain in my dream. There were lots of vehicles on the runway, also the plane had tipped on to its side. The local airport was Manchester. When I saw the picture in the paper, everything was exactly as in my dream; they could have taken a picture of my dream, it was so exact. And it was an Air Tours plane.

Mrs Y. Moore from Eastleigh, Hants, wrote:

I dreamt I was walking into Eastleigh over a railway bridge and a plane came down and crashed. Then I woke up. The next day, a plane had to do an emergency landing in Eastleigh. It had trouble with its wheels, but landed OK. I was walking into Eastleigh at the time.

Miss M. Lee of Durham had a preview of another air crash:

I dreamt I was standing looking out of a window. Outside of the window I saw water, just like the sea. The water was quite upset and I could hear the sea swirling. Suddenly the house started to vibrate and I ran to the back of the house where I saw a jet, flying really low above the house. I ran back through to the room and saw smoke coming from the jet as it headed towards the water. I heard men saying 'Get out' and in a really distressing voice 'We're going to crash!' Just at that moment one man parachuted out of the plane, then the plane hit the water. I suddenly woke up and told my mother about the dream. I also wrote it down. Three days later the news was on and my mother shouted to me. A story was on the news about a jet that had crashed into the sea, with one man surviving. I couldn't believe it: the dream was not exact, but I recognised the whole scene on TV from my dream!

Miss Lee also had a premonition dream about a car accident which was later reported on the news. In this accident, a car had crashed through a fence and had fallen down an embankment. There were casualties and only a baby survived. In the dream Miss Lee saw the above scene in great detail, again from a window. There was a small, unused, winding road; suddenly she saw a car speeding up, braking, and then toppling over a hill. She became aware of people shouting and searching for the baby, and somehow felt involved with this search. The next day, while on holiday in Wales, she woke up and switched on the radio only to hear of this very event.

Television is now the 'window to the world'. Television programmes, especially the news, can communicate to the masses one particular message, thereby connecting thoughts and ideas to the collective unconsciousness of people all around the world. The same applies to radio and, of course, the Internet! The dream state finds it easy to incorporate these methods of communication, especially when reporting important events.

Faith Hall, who lives in Gloucester, had a disturbing dream about the Lockerbie disaster, three days before it happened. She wrote:

> My only premonition dream happened three days before the Lockerbie disaster. In the dream I was with some other people and we seemed to be near a beach by the sea shore. Suddenly we saw, high up in the sky, some kind of aircraft (it didn't actually look like an aeroplane, more like a space ship), and it was hurtling down at great speed towards the ground. It was now very frightening. Then I seemed to be high up in the sky myself, looking down in horror as the aircraft hit the ground far below me with a dreadful impact and exploded into flames. Suddenly, coming from all directions towards the burning wreckage, I saw fire-engines, police cars and ambulances racing and forming a circle round the fire. Then I heard my own voice saying, in great grief: 'It's no good. They are all dead.'
>
> I was very shocked and bewildered by this dream and could not imagine why I had dreamt such a thing. (Normally my dreams are fairly prosaic – a sort of jumbled version of the day's experiences.) Only after three days did I hear about the tragic Lockerbie crash and I was stunned to realise the connection.

Quite a lot of women wrote to me of experiencing the same emotions as those of whom the dream was about, almost as if it's happening to you, although in the morning when you wake up you realise that the dream is about someone else. In the case of news events this is frustrating, because one is left with the feeling of 'I wish I could have helped or prevented it from happening'. Claire Flynn of Llandudno wrote:

> During my 'A' level exams, when I was under quite a lot of stress, I dreamt I was sitting in our sixth-form common room listening to a news report on the radio. I was suddenly at the Winter Olympics watching the downhill skiers. As a skier was coming downhill, he didn't see a snow plough cross the course, and crashed into it and died. When I woke the next morning, I was watching a TV report which detailed how a skier on a practice run had crashed into a snow plough and died.

Edna Wordsworth wrote to me of several dreams. This one concerns a radio news announcement:

> Early one Saturday morning, I dreamt that a terrorist bomb had gone off in the doorway of a nightclub just off Piccadilly, and I noticed that the bombers were of Middle Eastern appearance. I woke up and turned on the radio just in time for the 8 a.m. news. It started thus: 'A bomb has gone off in the doorway of a nightclub in Piccadilly.' Later in the day, we were told there was a Middle East connection.

Everyday Events

Some preview dreams concern quite commonplace events of a pleasant nature, relevant only to life at home. However, they are still previews of the future. Alison Hutchings wrote:

> I was a fan (and still am) of Simon and Garfunkel and I often wrote in to Radio Cornwall requesting their music. One day, I wrote in to them asking them to play two songs: 'The Boxer' and 'The Sound of Silence' in that order on their 'two in a row' spot which they did at 9.30 a.m. every day. I didn't specify which day, as I listened in every day. On Wednesday night I had a very vivid and detailed dream – I was having breakfast with my mother and we were

talking away. I didn't notice the time, but when I glanced at the clock I noticed it had gone past 9.30. I dashed upstairs to my room and switched on the radio. They were half-way through playing 'The Sound of Silence'. It turned out to be my request and I'd missed it! The following Saturday that is exactly what happened. I had breakfast with my Mum which took longer than usual. I ran upstairs, switched the radio on and they were half-way through playing my song! I remember feeling disappointed as I had done in my dream.

Susan Wood from London dreamt:

I had a dream that my friend was getting married and I was to be the bridesmaid. I was getting married in July, but in my dream my friend was getting married before me. She hadn't known her boyfriend long. The next day, she phoned with some news: I told her she was getting married before she had the chance to tell me!

Mrs D. Woolford wrote:

In my dream a friend I worked with had her long hair in a ponytail. The next day as I walked into work, she was looking very smart with it just as I had seen it in my dream.

Lisa Doolan from Scotland wrote of an outing to Livingston, with her school friend:

My dream involved me, my Mum and my friend Kay. We went to Livingston and met up with my aunt, uncle and two cousins. My cousin Sean was wearing a Celtic tracksuit and Andrea (my aunt) had just bought chips, pineapple rings and bacon. In the morning my Mum announced that she was going to Livingston and would we like to go? When we got there we bumped into everyone in my dream. Sean was wearing his new Celtic tracksuit and Chris was eating some kind of pastry with a pineapple ring on top. I explained my dream to them and Andrea told me she had just bought micro chips and gammon steaks for the dinner.

Mrs Ogilvie, an elderly lady from Falkirk, wrote of a similar unexpected excursion:

I dreamt I was on my way by car when I passed a kiosk selling papers. This was on a road heading to Glasgow which I knew. I saw a sign saying 'Erskine Ferry'. On waking on the Sunday morning I told my husband. At 9 a.m., whilst we were having breakfast, a friend called in and asked if we would like a surprise run as it was such a nice day. We set off at 12 noon. I soon noticed we were on the road which I had seen in my dream, then I saw the sign saying 'Erskine Ferry': my friend was taking us to see the QE2 at Erskine near the Clyde while it was in for a re-fit. I told her about my dream the previous night – I couldn't believe it!

World News Events

Mrs Jeane Dixon, the famous American seer (about 80 per cent of her predictions have been accurate), said that premonitions fall into two categories: divine revelation on the one hand, and more personal visions on the other. The former is definite and irrevocable, the latter tell of what is likely unless people intervene to change the outcome. The premonition dream accounts I have read tend to back this up. We shall see in the next chapter that some people were able to act on some of their warning dreams, but in the dreams of a forthcoming death people felt unable to act.

Continuing with previews, we now come to those of famous figures. There were, of course, a lot of warnings and premonition dreams about President Kennedy's assassination; in fact people did try to warn him of this, but he either didn't receive the messages or decided he couldn't spend his life walking on eggshells. Another interesting but disturbing fact is that historically it seemed like quite a likely event, because every President of the United States elected at twenty-year intervals has died in office: Abraham Lincoln, elected 1860, assassinated 1865; James Garfield, elected 1880, assassinated 1881; W. McKinley, elected 1900, assassinated 1901; Warren Harding, elected 1920, died 1923; Franklin D. Roosevelt, elected 1940, died 1945; John F. Kennedy, elected 1960, assassinated 1963; and President Ronald Reagan survived an assassination attempt in the 1980s.

Jean Holland, a practising dream therapist, wrote:

> I saw in a dream hundreds or thousands of Zulus marching in South Africa – they had spears and other weapons, as well as guns, and

some wore African tribal dress. This actually happened some time later when Inkatha members marched through Johannesburg to speak to Mr Mandela. The ANC thought they were trying to cause trouble, and people of both political parties started firing. When I saw it on TV, I realised I had seen the entire scene in my dream.

Mrs F. Lancaster from Durham dreamt:

I was looking at a photograph of President Abraham Lincoln. It said 'Abraham Lincoln, born 18– died 1960'. I couldn't understand it, as he'd been dead for years. Then, watching TV the following evening, at 7.30 a news flash came on to say that President Kennedy had been shot, elected 1960.

Mrs E. E. Smith of Portsmouth had the following dream:

I dreamt I was walking through a graveyard and on either side of the path I was walking on was a large tombstone. On each tombstone was the letter E. I woke up very upset, my name being Eileen Elizabeth. I thought this was the meaning of the two E.'s. That day, I had a tearful phone call from my mother-in-law to say her future husband Eddie had died. Later the same day, I heard on the news that my idol, Elvis, had died.

Mrs J. Priest of Coalville dreamt that Alec Douglas-Home would win the 1963 election and he did. She and a few of the other women to dream of political figures were not overly political themselves, and this peculiarity served to make their dreams stand out.
Mrs M. Stuart from Dorset wrote:

Some time ago I dreamed of the Labour leader John Smith. He was serving behind the counter in a shop; all the merchandise was black and I was surprised to see him in this place. He told me that I should change any red garments to black. Two weeks later John Smith died of a heart attack.

Mrs Stuart has also had previews of actual events, such as ambulances arriving for her neighbours. However, she wouldn't inform them of this as she wouldn't want to worry them. It is good to exercise wisdom and discretion if you have foresight. There is not always a tactful way of putting a warning message across if the person is to grasp the urgency of it, but then that is where all the sayings come from – 'Beware the Ides of March!'

Mrs E. Bowers from Stafford dreamt that President Gorbachev was going to be shot twice by an assassin:

> I was obviously concerned as there was nothing I could do to stop this. Nothing happened, then two years later a young man was arrested with information and articles suggesting that he had been planning to murder President Gorbachev. It later transpired that he began this plot two years earlier, around the time of my dream.

Mrs J.G. of Rochdale saw what she later realised to be the Hillsborough disaster. Most of it was symbolic.

> I saw a long train pull into the station and stop. A large crowd of people got off. Then I saw a close-up shot of one carriage; it was empty but for a body and a football. The picture vanished, and I fell asleep. When I woke up, the picture re-appeared just as before, as if I were watching a television screen. I saw a long line of hearses carrying coffins queuing to pass through a large pair of wrought iron gates. Over the top of the gates it said 'Cemetery'. Then the picture disappeared.

Mrs G. did not understand the dream until a news flash came on that afternoon.

This was one of Mrs G.'s earlier experiences and she wished she had been more tuned in then as she is now, so that she could have passed the message on; but, as she said, 'Would anyone have believed me?' And this is the nature of some premonitions: football matches occur every week with no problems, so our common sense and logic assume that it would be safe to go and watch a favourite team playing.

Mrs J. Richards from Norfolk wrote to me about the cruise liner *Queen Elizabeth*:

> I had a dream in which I could see the *Queen Elizabeth* listing very badly. People were jumping off the liner into the water. It was so real that even when I woke up the dream was still with me. As I had had premonition dreams before, I was very concerned. I wanted to tell

the liner's owners but they would probably have thought I was some sort of crank, so I decided after a couple of days to write to the *Daily Mirror*. Of course I heard nothing from them, despite giving as much information as I could. In 1969, the liner was taken out of service and I thought nothing more about it – although I wouldn't have gone on a cruise on it myself if asked! Then in 1972 I was watching the news when I saw the *Queen Elizabeth* listing and workmen jumping over the side into the water. The annoying thing about this dream was that it took so long to come true, and one is often left with the feeling 'What if?' 'If I had managed to contact the right people could this have been avoided?'

Experience shows that, nine times out of ten, people go their own way and accidents like this happen when you least expect them. Even if you are prepared, it's no guarantee that you will escape the situation, especially if there are long time gaps between the warning and the actual event. For example, someone once warned me most intently to be careful when driving on the roads because of lorries and tractors. So of course I was, but the weeks went by and I relaxed my vigilance. I went to pick up my friend's dog from the country as I was looking after it while they went away. As I left I had the overwhelming feeling to stay and chat for a bit longer, but my willpower overtook my intuition and I got into the car and drove down the track instead. As I approached the junction I thought that all was clear, so I continued to drive, right into the path of a tractor! Fortunately I had my seatbelt on and the dog, Juno, was OK because he had jumped into the front of the car with me. The car needed quite a lot of repair though!

Chapter V

Warning Dreams

Many warning dreams have a sense of urgency that stays with the person when they wake up. The person dreaming may have had a warning dream either for themselves or for other people. In my survey only 20 per cent of people were able to act on their warnings, thereby avoiding danger. In each case, the person involved was extra vigilant during the following days, and so ensured that the undesirable event could be avoided. I'd like to start with examples of those dreams in which a warning was heeded, and the dreamer successfully avoided their 'fate'.

First is Mrs P.R., whose boyfriend had recently died:

In the dream, I was in my friend Simon's living room. The phone rang, and after a short but friendly chat Simon passed the phone to me saying it was Bob. There was background noise like a party. He said he was with his family now and was happy. The message he wanted to get across was one of concern – he wanted to let me know he was worried for my safety in my car. This was communicated to me in thoughts, rather than words, and relayed in such a way that expressed his distress and grave concern for my welfare. The next scene showed my car badly smashed in on the driver's side, and that it was 'idiots' that did it.

Next morning going to work I was very careful, as there was ice on the sides of the road, and I was mindful of my dream. I arrived at work unscathed. On my way home, thinking about my dream, I was still very cautious on the side roads. When I got on the main road I thought I'd be all right. It was pitch black and I was doing about 60 mph. I turned a bend and then another, and I saw two sets of headlights a short distance in front of me. I immediately knew this was the situation I had been warned of, and swerved into the gutter. The car went by me so close – we were three abreast – and I'm sure he clipped my wing mirror! I pulled in further up to check, and was extremely shaken up by my near miss which, had I not been so vigilant, could have been very serious; my car was indeed bashed in on the driver's side, just as the dream had portrayed.

Many people have triggers which then recall the warning dream scenario; as soon as one recognises the warning sign, it is important to act on it.

Mrs E.B. of Stafford wrote:

> I dreamt my friend cut his arm badly in a farming accident. I told him about it the next day, and he laughed about it. The next day he very nearly lost some fingers in a piece of machinery which he'd used carefully for many years. He later said he'd been aware of my dream all day, and would certainly have had an accident if he hadn't been aware of some danger from my dream.

Elizabeth Ross-Fraser from north-east Scotland wrote:

> I had a warning dream not to go on a sleeper train. Next day, despite having a prior sleeper reservation, I decided to postpone my journey from Inverness to London, and travel during the day instead. The next morning I learned that 'my' train had crashed outside London at Harrow and Wealdstone, with a loss of over 300 lives.

Ms Ross-Fraser is a generally intuitive person, and has had other supernatural experiences. She is also considerate, intelligent and has a sense of humour, qualities which all seem to go along with having a sixth sense.

Miss T.L. wrote:

> When I was young, I dreamed I was knocked down by an orange car. I told a school friend of mine, and for several days we joked on our way to school if we saw an orange car. While crossing the road I was daydreaming, and walked on to the road. I looked up and saw a car moving slowly. The driver and I both paused, then I continued to walk and the car drove forward, hitting me. Fortunately, my leg was only bruised, and I was more concerned that it was an orange car! The driver was naturally quite upset, and it turned out that she had had the same dream as me!

This next experience was quite unexpected. In my opinion, we can rule out the possibility of telepathy or coincidence, as the person in question tried to avoid her fate. Joyce Hudson wrote:

Warning Dreams

I dreamt I was on a train, when all of a sudden the guard came running up the aisle, shouting 'Fire! Fire!' Everyone was in a panic. The train stopped, and I ran to the door. I opened it and jumped out. I looked back and saw the engine on fire and some elderly people trying to get out. I ran back and helped them off. One lady was most upset. She kept saying 'My suitcase, my suitcase, I want my suitcase!' 'Leave it, don't worry about it', I said. I helped three people off, and we all ran across a field. Then I woke up. Now, I had no intentions of going out that day. Later, a friend came down and asked if I would go to Cleethorpes with her on the bus. I told my friend about my dream. When we got to the bus station, we were told that there was a strike, so we went by train. All was well on the journey there. We'd had a long day, and were shattered when we returned, and I'd forgotten all about my dream. Then it happened. The guard started to shout 'Fire! Fire!' and we all managed to get off the train as predicted in my dream.

It seemed that the women who had more experience of premonitions were more able to act on information received in their dreams. Having said that, a person was much more likely to avoid a situation if it happened immediately after the warning, or only a day later! Nearly all the women who wrote to me had extrasensory perception of some sort during the day as well – most commonly telepathy, or a feeling of 'knowing' something was about to happen.

Miss P. McKissack from London had a dream that her neighbour's house was on fire. The neighbour had a three-year-old daughter, and everyone was looking for her. In the dream, the fire had taken hold of the entire house. Miss McKissack could not remember the ending of the dream. Then, about a year later, she was woken up in the early hours by her mother telling her that the neighbour's house was on fire. Fortunately, the three-year-old and her mother were safe, and the fire was eventually put out by the Fire Brigade.

Miss A.R. had a dream that her son was being robbed. Two days later she phoned her son to warn him, but he said it had already happened!

There is an idea that we all have parallel destinies; if we act on a premonition dream, thus avoiding death or danger, we can follow our parallel destiny, but if we do not act we continue on our original line of fate. Mario de Sabato, a famous French clairvoyant (born 1933), believed in 'parallel destinies', in which we can alter our likely destinies by an act of will – the future is not always fixed. However, if we fail to make necessary changes after being forewarned of something, then the event takes place anyway, as predicted. Dr Michael Newton, author of *Destiny of Souls*, tells how patients could recall viewing parallel options of their futures if they missed the reminders/cues – if, at a crossroads point in life, they took a different, or wrong, turning from the one which had been pre-arranged (as we all have free will). If something is meant to happen, then for our destiny to be fulfilled it will still happen, but it may occur at a later date, or in a more roundabout way.

Mario de Sabato's principal concern, like that of many people who are naturally psychic, was to love humanity. He was also a devoutly religious and spiritual person. Most of his prophecies came true.

Chapter VI

Dreams of Death

Many people dreamt of the forthcoming death of relatives, friends or even associates. This chapter concerns itself with the accounts and experiences of those who have died and been resuscitated, followed by the premonition dreams of women. My aim is to encourage people to have hope for the future and to strengthen their beliefs in life after death. I believe that death is not a random event, as it sometimes appears, but is well arranged, pre-arranged even, and the prophetic dreams of women would back this up. Just as the universe has order, so it is with our passing over to the spiritual world. This last event has been well documented throughout the world and has stood the test of time. Should we try to have a more positive view of death? – seeing it as a transition from one state to another? Should we, if possible, face it bravely, with calmness and dignity? – with hope, trust and interest in this, the closing chapter of the life we have known and lived? Looking forward to the emergence of a new form of life? Or do we pass into it without hope?

Edgar Cayce met a beautiful angel and discovered he was the angel of death. 'People don't expect death to be a beautiful experience', he said, 'but it is'.

Many religions talk of a physical body and a spirit within man. It has been reported that when death occurs, the spirit leaves the body and soars up to God who is experienced as a presence of love, knowledge, peace and joy. Many people report being in the presence of an intensely Bright Light which is All Knowing, yet emanates Love. I use capitals because these are aspects of God; when a person encounters God, he feels the power of Love and then receives an illumination of the spirit. Clarity is clearly there, when connecting to the story of one's life.

There are many accounts of people meeting the Light between dying and being resuscitated in Dr Peter and Elizabeth Fenwick's book *The Truth in the Light*.

Most esoteric teachings acknowledge the light; for example, before meditation, New Age followers will first of all cover themselves in the light as a form of protection. Light can be seen in auras;

this can be used as a connection between the material world and the spiritual world.

In the Bible, Jesus is referred to as the 'Light of the World' and as having great compassion. In the Tibetan Book of the Dead we can find instructions for the spirit of a man as he makes his journey into the spiritual afterlife. The ultimate advice they give is: 'When you see a Bright Light, go to the Light' and 'When you see the Lord of Great Compassion go to Him.' Most religions believe in life after death, and until now the personal experience of this has remained in the domain of mystics. This is because these experiences were subjective and not open to any scientific investigation. Now, in the twenty-first century, the new age of Aquarius, a transformation has taken place. A breakthrough has come about with the advent of new technology where we have mass resuscitation (resurrection) of patients who have temporarily died in hospital, usually in the operating theatre.

Dr Peter Fenwick of the Maudsley hospital in London, and co-author of *The Truth in the Light*, noted that of ten patients who died of cardiac arrest, one was revived and reported an out-of-body experience. Dr Fenwick and two of his colleagues, Margot Grey and David Lorimer, decided to carry out some research into this – purely because so many people were talking about it. The results of the survey showed that 'dead' patients saw a Light which was full of love. The Light was all encompassing and infused the 'deceased' person with His presence of Peace, Love and Joy. They said that the Light had an identity but they could not see any form. They felt so happy in the Light's presence that they did not wish to return to their bodies at all. Some patients were able to describe what was going on in the hospital after having been pronounced dead: this means that they were not hallucinating (as some scientists would argue). So the question is, 'If the soul can survive the body after death for a few seconds why not for a few minutes ... why not for eternity?'

It seems, then, that prior to death, some relatives or even the person themselves will become aware that they are about to die; this happens either through a premonition dream which includes an element of certainty, or through intuition. The deceased person then goes on his or her journey towards a more blissful place. I would like to include here a quotation from Peter Fenwick's book *The Truth in the Light*:

Dreams of Death

> For most people the near death experience is one of the most profound they will ever have. It is vividly remembered for years – often for a whole lifetime. (p. 16)

Dr Raymond Moody, in his book *Life After Life*, says (from his investigations) that the spirit of the dying man encounters a being of Light who asks him questions telepathically, and at the same time the spirit sees a panoramic view of his previous life. The spirit then evaluates the decisions he made while alive on the earth, and can see where he may have erred or done well. It is widely reported that most people who return from this kind of experience decide to become less self-centred and more caring of others, realising that there is an underlying moral code in the universe. This moral code ideally operates from a standpoint of love rather than enforced rules and regulations, grace rather than judgement. I would like to give the analogy of a cyclist: you are driving a car along the road, and you see an old man riding a bike. You overtake, giving him plenty of space. You do this out of love so that the man will not be hurt by falling off his bike, and so that you yourself will not be emotionally hurt as you would be if the man was injured. There are laws to protect the vulnerable; these laws enforce the above level of respect. Some people would show courtesy/respect out of consideration and others out of obeying the law. Which would you prefer? Love is the answer. People who return from an encounter with the Light end up looking for vocations rather than purely money-oriented jobs, or they will try to do some vocational work over and above their usual type of employment. They find that they are bringing down the Light, in one way or another.

Many spiritually aware people are, of course, loving and kind on a daily basis irrespective of their physical or material situation.

Some people who die and are brought back to life again recall being shown glimpses of their future as they return to their bodies. These previews then begin to unfold with the passage of time. According to the accounts in Raymond Moody's book, the reviews and previews of one's life were shown in a very non-judgemental way.

I would like to include another short extract from Raymond Moody's book, *Life After Life*, which to me illustrates that animals also have a soul:

The Future in Your Dreams

Shortly before his death in 1951, Jean Johnstone's father told her of a wonderful dream:

He dreamt that he had been walking along the foothills of the Himalayas where he had once worked. As he did so, all his pet dogs came to greet him, wagging their tails, whilst the sun grew brighter and brighter behind the mountains. He felt strong and happy, and was disappointed to hear that he had to 'go back'.

The old gentleman told his daughter about the dream, and died shortly after. The universal symbol of light in a dream indicates wisdom, learning, knowledge or understanding. It is also (in this case) reminiscent of the Light encountered in near-death experiences.

It will be comforting to animal lovers to know that a few of the women who wrote to me also dreamt of their pet's death before it happened. These dreams were in the minority: nevertheless, I thought it would be right to include them here, animals being our best friends at times. There is often some doubt in some people's minds as to whether animals have an afterlife. It seems from these premonition dreams that they do. For example, Denise Hill, a housewife from Birmingham, wrote: 'Once I dreamt my dog died and five days later he became sick and died although he had been perfectly healthy previously.'

Miss A.H. also had a dream that her dog had been run over by a car and was lying on a grass verge next to the road. The next day while out for a walk, this is just what happened.

Finally, my daughter had a cat, called Oscar. One night I dreamt that my daughter and I went on a journey in a 1950s single-decker bus. A large prehistoric bird flew overhead across some yellow-coloured fields. When we got off the bus, we went in through the door of a house and found ourselves in a farmhouse kitchen. A retired American cop came in with Oscar. The cop said in a kindly voice, 'It's O.K. I'll look after him now.' He stroked Oscar, who then went and drank from a blue and white bowl of milk. That was the end of the dream. In the morning, I was puzzled by this dream, although quite often symbolic dreams of death contain a bird messenger, at least in my own dreams. Then, three days later, we received a phone call to say that Oscar had been knocked down on the main road and killed.

Many people wrote to me of being forewarned of a death. A lot of women felt that this helped to soften the blow when they eventually heard the news. Dreams of a forthcoming death can be transmitted in various ways. Sometimes live or deceased relatives will appear in the dream. Sometimes the dreamer is present themselves. But in most cases the person had a preview of the way in which they were to learn about the death. Those who heard of a death by telephone would dream of the telephone conversation, or by letter, of a letter, and so on. The death in a dream is seen in the present: it is not until the person wakes up that they realise that their friend or relative is still alive. Some people would pick up on some telltale signs of the time of death while others would have a déjà vu experience which would then trigger off the rest of the dream on the day they heard of the death. Following are some accounts of women's premonition dreams of a forthcoming death.

H. Thomas wrote:

> I dreamt that I was standing round a hospital bed with my family looking at my Dad. I knew he was seriously ill and that his death was imminent. Several weeks later my father was indeed admitted to hospital and the family were called to see him; the next day my father died.

Several women wrote to me of seeing a late family member in a dream coming to collect a loved one as it was their time to go. Most of my own dreams of someone who is about to die are symbolic, but I learnt to recognise the symbology over a short space of time. Perhaps my subconscious mind prefers to use birds and the like as a way of softening the blow. The bird, according to Jung, is a beneficial animal which represents spirits or angels and supernatural assistance. Strangely, people from ancient civilisations, for example the ancient Egyptians, Aztecs and Romans, used bird symbols as an omen of death. Romany Gypsies thought of owls as death birds.

We can all learn of a forthcoming event in different ways. One or two women heard of a loved one's death via a letter. A lovely lady, Win Nott of Surrey, had a very special penfriend called Eddie, whom she corresponded with. Then one night she had a dream:

> In my dream I saw a letter in our box addressed to Mrs W. in a strange hand. I felt a sense of foreboding. Later that day I went to our letterbox. There was the letter, addressed to Mrs W. – and in a

strange hand. I opened it with foreboding – the feeling I had in my dream! The letter was from Eddie's sister telling me that he had died. She did not know my surname. It is a dream which left such an impression, I have never forgotten it.

Premonition dreams do leave a lasting impression and this, plus their clarity, is what distinguishes them from ordinary dreams.

Another lady had a dream of a letter being handed to her. Mrs Jean R.B. from Scotland had a dream about her husband Laurence. In her dream, her husband was wading in from the sea with a letter in his hand; he handed the letter to Jean, saying he was so sorry. Mrs Jean R.B. woke up perplexed as her husband was a very good swimmer. She also had a sense of foreboding in her dream. The next day, Mrs Jean R.B. received a telegram to say that her husband was missing, presumed drowned. He had decided to swim to the shore from a yacht in Arabia, before having lunch, but he was never seen again.

Many believe that it is possible for people who have died to visit their loved ones in their dreams. There is further information about this in the next chapter, in the section on astral dreams.

A young housewife, Angela Wellington, wrote:

I went to bed and dreamt that I had seen a white mini crashing. It was so vivid: I was standing at the side watching, but couldn't move to help anybody. I felt such sadness as I sensed who was in the car but could not see their face. I told my mother and just couldn't get it out of my mind. Then, a few days later, an ex-boyfriend got killed in a white mini just as I had dreamt it. Three years later, I felt I ought to go up to the cemetery with some flowers. I wrote a card out in ink. That night there was a terrible storm, so the next day I went back to the grave with a new card and to rearrange the flowers. When I got there, all the other flowers and wreaths had blown everywhere but mine was still in the centre, where I had lain them, and the card was dry.

Mrs Webster dreamt about the death of her father (born 18.8.18):

My husband and I went to bed quite late. During the night I woke up feeling very frightened and shook my husband. 'Ozzie,' I said, 'I just dreamt of my father dead!' He was in a coffin with a purple robe.

My husband told me not to be silly and to go back to sleep. Six months later my father died.

Mrs Webster continued to dream about her father for six to twelve months after his death, which is also common to most bereaved people.

Mrs J. Curthoys from Newcastle-upon-Tyne also saw her father in a coffin in a dream. She was very upset by this and felt a deep sorrow. This was to let her know of what was to occur later that year, and her feelings were identical to the ones in her dream. Mrs Curthoys also believes that her dreams indicate whether she can intervene or not: the dream of her father's death was fated, whereas other everyday events could be altered by an act of will. Dreams that could be altered tended to contain more detail and were recurring, compared to dreams of a person's death.

Mrs S. Price wrote:

I dreamt that my uncle had a chest infection and was house-bound. My cousin came over with his supper one night; he was sitting in his favourite chair in the front room, with his pipe in his mouth, listening to his favourite music. In the dream I could hear the music and smell his pipe as if I were actually there. He clutched his chest, slumped in the chair and was dead. A short time later, my cousin arrived with his meal and knocked on the door, but there was no answer, so she let herself in and found my uncle had died. Six months later, the dream came true. My cousin phoned up to speak to my father, and I went into the kitchen and told my mother about the dream. I was told not to be so silly! Once father was off the phone, my dream was verified.

Mrs Price also had many other premonition dreams about the death of a family member. They were exact replicas of the actual event and the cause of death was foreseen even though the relatives did not have the symptoms: for example, one of her aunts died suddenly of a brain haemorrhage. Other dreams detailed the funeral and the guests who would attend. Many people find it a great comfort to know that things are being prepared for them, and (here I agree with the other dreamers) it helps take the shock out of the announcement when it actually happens. It also means that we can go and pay our respects while the person is still here,

The Future in Your Dreams

although I always try to do that anyway – I have learnt that putting things off for even one day can make such a monumental difference. Usually I would feel a draw to visit the person while awake as well as in the dream state. Mrs Price has had premonition dreams from a very early age, which was common to many of the people who wrote to me.

Mrs Kelly of West Sussex dreamt of her husband's colleague's death at around the time of it happening: she told her husband about the dream. Then at 9.30 that morning, her husband phoned to tell her that his colleague had been killed in a road accident during the early hours of the morning. Mrs Kelly also dreamt that her son's teacher had died, and several days later her son arrived home from school early because of this.

Mrs Smith of Lancashire dreamt that her Sunday School teacher had died, and three days later she heard that the lady had died after a short illness. Mrs Smith also dreamt that her bridesmaid, still young, had died, so when she heard that her friend was still alive, she felt relieved; however, three months later she died as predicted in the dream. All the dreams mentioned above were dreamt as if in the present.

Pamela Goodwin from Wrexham had a dream about her Sunday School teacher too:

> A year after my mother died, she appeared to me in a very real dream, sitting on my bed. She said that my old Sunday School teacher – who also played the organ at my wedding – would get in touch with me the next day, needing my help. Mum also said that this lady's husband would die in three days' time. I had not heard from my old Sunday School teacher since the time of my wedding. The next day she did indeed phone and told me that her husband had been in hospital, but was coming out and could I help her by giving her some phone numbers of mutual church friends? I then heard that her husband had died unexpectedly, three days after my dream.

Mrs Goodwin also dreamt of her father's forthcoming death.

It is interesting to note that, like myself, many of the women who have dreams about the future are actually of the Christian faith. This only goes to show that we shouldn't go around 'pigeon holing' each other because of our various beliefs: some beliefs and ideas do actually overlap.

Dreams of Death

Jean Rogers of Darlington wrote:

> One night I dreamt my late grandfather came downstairs and went into the front room where my father was ill. He took my father's hand and said 'come on son, it's time'. He led my father upstairs to the landing and they both disappeared through the stained glass window. My father died a couple of days later.

Sometimes a dream may give information of a death, by the noticeable absence of a person in the dream. This helps to break the news more gently to the dreamer. In the three days before my grandfather died, I had three dreams (one on each night). In the first dream, my husband died; in the second dream, my father died; and in the third one, my father-in-law died. The scene was always the same: our family were congregated in the living room (in-laws and all) when the news was broken to us. The next day, my Norwegian grandparents were to meet my new in-laws for the first time. My grandfather had gone out for a walk before lunch. Soon after, my in-laws arrived and we were all congregated in the living room; just then, the police came to the door to say that my grandfather had died.

Soon after this, I had a dream in which I was visited by my grandfather. He showed me the new area where I was about to live and introduced me to my new friends, whom I was to meet at a party. Sure enough, several weeks later, my life had competely changed around and I did indeed meet the people in my dream; even though a lot of them were new to me, I recognised them by their clothes and the setting. The house was also refreshingly correct (i.e. corresponding to my dream) and I felt very happy, because that period of time was one of my best. All this followed on from quite a difficult patch for me, so it was a most welcome relief.

Mrs Griffiths of Preston had a similar dream in which the person dying was missing in the dream:

> I remember having a dream which always stayed clearly with me over the years. It would have been two years after my husband Martin's death in a car accident. In my dream I was reliving the morning of his funeral. I can remember looking out of the window for a funeral car. All my family were with me, exactly as it was on

the day, two years previously. Then I recall saying that the hearse was coming up the street, so we had all better get ourselves ready to leave. To my dismay, the hearse did not come to our house, but to the house opposite me. When I looked out of the window, the couple from across the road and their two daughters all came out of their house. They were all dressed in black and got into the hearse. It was then that I noticed that the grandmother wasn't there. And it was at this point that I realised that it was the grandmother's funeral.

Mrs Griffiths told her son about her dream, then one week later, her son called in to say that the old grandmother from across the road had died.

One day, I was looking out of the window of my house and I saw three young men who were helping to build a house across the road. The sun was shining brightly and there was a breeze which blew the hair away from their faces. The sunlight highlighted their glowing faces and brought out a myriad of colours in their hair. They were laughing and joking and slapping each other on the back. I thought 'ah, the splendour and carefreeness of youth'. Something about them and the light stood out and I couldn't get the image out of my mind. I told my sister about it in the morning; her face went ashen and her eyes widened. She said: 'Yes, they were my boyfriend's friends, but ... they were all killed last night as their van crashed into a tree.' I mention this because since then I have noticed that often there is a special glow or a golden tint around people before they go.

The last time I saw my father alive, there was such a wonderful unforgettable atmosphere, a lightness in the room, and there seemed to be a sense of timelessness. Even though it was getting late, there was a warm glow from the late sunshine in the room. We had a wonderful time together, and it comforts me to have had such a good parting. Later, when my father did die abroad, I had a symbolic dream of an eagle coming over the sea with the sunlight on its back. All the colours in its feathers were illuminated and the eagle swept down majestically, wing feathers tipped upwards. The eagle brought me a message and then flew away slowly, silently and sombrely, back in the direction from whence it had come, Spain. When I woke up I knew what the dream meant; even though others around me were saying that my father was all right, he wasn't – he died (unexpectedly) seven days later, in hospital.

Many people dream of birds as the harbingers of death: for example, the eagle can represent the father, and crows in like manner could symbolise the death of the person in the dream. As with all symbols, once it is connected frequently enough with the actual event in the waking world, then that symbol is correct for you. That is, if one dreams of a particular type of bird in association with a friend or relative, and then that person dies, it soon becomes apparent that symbolically that bird represents someone's passing into spirit world. I had a dream where a person I knew was being attacked by a buzzard; at first I was behaving like a passive viewer, but then I consciously decided to intervene within the dream. I shot the bird; the bird died and the person recovered. The next day I had a telephone call saying that the person I had just dreamt about had been under a physical and mental attack, but that they had been rescued and taken to hospital; they were in intensive care, but made a remarkable recovery. Was this the meaning of the dream? Personally I believe so.

Some premonition dreams are symbolic, some are lucid. Lucid dreams are ones in which one can alter things consciously in the dream, while dreaming. Another way to control the dream is to write down how you would have liked the dream to be, how to solve the problem presented to you in the dream. This may help greatly with recurring dreams. For example, you keep having to go down the same corridor in the dream; you try to escape, but the doors are locked. Every time, the same. Just try writing that next time, three of the doors are going to be open, so that you have a choice of which door to choose. Then see if it affects the real-life situation. I know it sounds superstitious, but there does seem to be a link between what goes on in a lucid dream and what goes on in real life: changing the dream event corresponds with changing the real-life event.

Mrs F.B. was ill for a while and she kept having to go into hospital. She became seriously ill and was very concerned about this. Then she started having dreams about being at a bus stop and getting on buses. One night, she linked the buses with impending bad news regarding her illness. She decided not to get on the first bus, or the second or the third, just to stand at the bus stop and let them all go by. Other people were getting on the buses; the bus waited for her, but when she stepped back, the bus drove off and she was still at the bus stop. After that her hospital visits stopped, because her health had greatly improved.

The most common premonition dreams will need no interpretation at all because they are in fact a preview of the actual event. It is for the dreamer to decide which category his or her dream falls into. Usually the dreamer knows, because over the passage of time a pattern will have emerged which separates the premonition dream from an ordinary escapism type of dream.

Rev. Wilda B. Tanner in her book *The Mystical Magical Marvelous World Of Dreams* says that it is possible to have conversations with our relatives in a dream as we can enter (spiritually) into the same astral plane as them. Thus it is possible to ask for or to give forgiveness to a deceased friend or relative, as well as gaining relevant insights from them.

Chapter VII

Telepathic Dreams

I did not receive many letters about telepathic dreams but there has been some research into this phenomenon. Telepathic dreams are communications between two people while one or both are asleep. Research carried out in America shows that it is possible to communicate pictures telepathically to dreaming subjects – most of these people were naturally psychic in their daily lives as well. For example, in an experiment carried out by Dr S. Krippner (Maimonides Dream Laboratory) in Brooklyn, New York, a psychic, Malcolm Bessent, slept overnight in the dream laboratory. The experiment included an audience who telepathically sent Mr Bessent a mental picture of the seven coloured chakras in the human body (the natural energy centres). This image was accurately picked up in Malcolm Bessent's dream. The dream included all the different colours of the chakras, corresponding to the rainbow colours: red, orange, yellow, green, blue, indigo, and violet purple, in ascending order.

In the UK several studies were carried out by psychologists Saul and Bateman with Gloria Stewart. She accurately predicted the patterns on specially designed cards (printed with simple shapes such as circle, square etc.): the experimenter viewed the cards first and then Mrs Stewart tuned in telepathically in order to gain the relevant information. Gloria consistently scored above average in these telepathic experiments.

Interestingly, it was found that subjects with a positive attitude to the possibility of telepathy scored much higher than those with negative views on the subject. This definitely reinforces the benefits of having faith in one's own abilities: if you have telepathic skills, keep believing in them and keep looking out for them!

The Ganzfeld Experiment set out to prove that certain people can use extrasensory perception. Scientist Professor Robert Morris and his colleagues at the Koestler Institute at Edinburgh University carried out an experiment whereby senders would send images (chosen randomly by computers) to a person in an enclosed cubicle. The cubicle was soundproof and had no windows so the receiver could not pick up on clues. The room was electromagnetically screened too, yet 50 per cent of those taking part in the experiment had a 'hit rate', choosing the correct images which had been 'sent' out to them. This was quite a good result considering that we are not really encouraged to use our ESP skills in general.

Another common feature of telepathic phenomena was the emotional states of the sender and receiver. For optimum results, the sender would have to be in an emotionally aroused state, while the receiver would be in an extremely relaxed state. This is why the dream state is such a good receptor for telepathic information. Some of the people who wrote to me about foreseeing the sex of their friends' babies were actually receiving this information at the same time as the birth of the child. This could suggest a case of astral projection during the dream, or telepathically receiving the enthusiastic news during the dream state. If the experience was one of astral projection, one would be likely to have the sensation of moving rapidly through the air and would possibly recall seeing oneself asleep. Otherwise, just straightforward telepathy, a mental ability, is likely.

There have been a few explanations for telepathy down the ages. The seventeenth-century philosopher René Decartes put forward a theory of memory that involved the possibility of thoughts being transferred by liquid through pores. The more often the liquid flows in a certain direction the more likely it would be for it to happen again. Modern psychological research indicates that certain 'logogens' are activated in the brain every time a particular word is used; the more often one uses this word the less time it takes to recall it (firing the appropriate lexicon). When these processes are observed in a photograph, we can see that the synaptic connections in the brain become modified as nerve signals pass through them, making it easier for the thought signals to flow through and be understood. Is it possible that others can pick up on these general thought waves?

I believe that thoughts are airborne, for want of a better word, because I have noticed that certain environments have a great influence on one's mental state. For example, while at University it seemed no effort at all for my mind to absorb information and I became more articulate when studying there than when in a more mundane environment. Perhaps my brain was being sharpened up by those around me. When working in a psychiatric hospital I noticed that quite a lot of the patients had been psychiatric nurses

– was this purely a coincidence? Or were they receptive to the air waves of a certain way of thinking? Are certain people drawn to that type of work? Perhaps, but I can say that just as the atmosphere in the University affected me so did the one in the hospital – and elsewhere. The list is quite long, so I won't go on. (We are wandering off into another area now, of sensing atmospheres, just another facet of our wonderfully powerful minds.)

It seems that the more one exercises telepathy and intuition, the stronger the ability becomes. A lot of it comes down to having faith and trusting in your own senses, listening to that inner voice, your intuition, your feelings. In this chapter I would like to include some interesting facts about telepathic communications between animals, but firstly, some intriguing accounts of telepathic dreams.

Mrs E. Wordsworth, a retired deputy headmistress, wrote:

I dream that I am travelling with three friends (I don't know who they are!) in a car, in South Wales – a place I had never been before. As we approach the outskirts of a small town, I tell the others I have a curious feeling that I can foretell what the road ahead will look like. I describe a grey stone house (L-shaped) at the right-angled bend in the road, and say that it will be covered in pink roses. I describe the sloping village street with the differently tiled roofs stretching downwards, and that we will pass a post office with the name of the village on a long sign. It will read 'Dowlais Post Office'. All this then happens as I have described it, but it's only a dream.

Three weeks later I go back to school. I'm sitting in the staff room when the Head of Languages asks the teacher of French where he went for his summer holidays. He then recounted details of his trip to South Wales with three friends in a car. 'While I was there,' he said, 'I had a very strange experience – I was able to describe the road ahead and an L-shaped building covered with pink roses on a bend.' By this time, a cold shiver had gone down my spine. He went on recounting how he had predicted the variegated sloping tiled roofs and the post office, and it was Dowlais, a place he'd never visited. The people around were amazed that I had dreamed this and he had predicted it while awake. We narrowed the coincidence down to a three-day period, but were not sure of the exact day. When I met him at a staff reunion twelve years later, I was introduced to his wife who said, 'You're the lady who shared the supernatural experience with my husband.' What was odd was that we were not close friends at all.

Many years later I went to Dowlais, but there were no roofs down the hill, only car parks, etc., etc., but in a TV programme about urban blight, the presenter quoted Dowlais and lamented 'the loss of the wonderful slate roofs with all their different colours'!

Mrs Wordsworth has also had other supernatural experiences and she comes across as a lively and interesting person, which research suggests are some of the qualities that telepathic dreamers have.

Mrs Galleymone of East Sussex wrote:

> My husband worked in a local hotel. One night I dreamed that I left the hotel and walked up the road, and the 'corridor maid' called to me from the other side, so I crossed over and spoke to her. Afterwards, I crossed back again. A car was coming towards me; the driver was a cousin I had not seen for some time, though we were very close during the war. He stopped the car and I got in. He said he had been searching for me. The very next day it happened exactly! The first thing I said was, 'I dreamed all this last night!' This happened in 1952, when he was a well-known violinist leading the Royal Orchestra at Glyndebourne.

This dream would have been a prearranged event, which could have been prompted by telepathic communication. Sir, if you are reading this, Mrs Galleymone (Cecilia) would like to hear from you again!

Mrs V. Corke from Kent had this telepathic dream:

> My husband's godfather was ill, and one Sunday I had a dream about him. I was napping, and I dreamed he came and kissed me on the cheek and put his hand on my shoulder. The event was so real that I told my family. We were all worried about him. The following day, my brother-in-law rang to say that godfather's wife had died on Sunday. My husband's godfather had been trying to ring us, but had lost the number.

Mrs Corke also knows telepathically when someone is going to visit her: 51 per cent of the women whose dreams come true said they had similar telepathic experiences themselves. For example,

Telepathic Dreams

Mrs J.S. from Suffolk wrote: 'I dreamt my aunt rang me about something she wanted me to do for her. Two days later she rang and said every single word that I dreamed she would say!' Was this telepathy?

Animal Magic

Animals in the wild, for example lions and tigers, have no problem using extrasensory perception (ESP) for protection; even spiders use cues that tell them when to move and not to move. Many animals can detect an earthquake coming, or refuse to enter a haunted room. Indeed, a survey involving pets showed that dogs knew when their owners were returning home. The owners would be sent to a restaurant and receive instructions to return home at an unspecified time. When they stood up, so did their pet dogs, who had been left at home; some of them even ran over to the window wagging their tails!

I, like many others, believe that dolphins communicate telepathically. There have been many reports of this from people who have worked with dolphins. I too have experienced them communicating with me while I was out in Spain. There was a show that involved dolphins and once it was over, I went to stand beside these dolphins at the pool's edge. Despite the fact that these beautiful serene creatures were confined in quite a small swimming space, they exuded happiness, wisdom and love. It may sound silly to anyone who hasn't worked with dolphins, but I felt appreciated and understood by them. They made a big impression on me, and it was a very moving experience. They don't just send out thoughts, they send out healing.

In another survey it seems that birds communicate via some etheric network. Once upon a time they didn't peck at milk bottle lids to get a sip of milk, and then all of a sudden thousands simultaneously started to peck through milk bottle lids right across Europe despite having had no physical contact with each other . . . how did they do that?

Asterix (my 'cosmic' cat) was an independent tom cat, and so tended to go off on journeys from time to time, either looking for adventure or because he had found some other interested 'owner' who loved cats! I would get quite worried about him sometimes.

During these times, I dreamt of Asterix returning to my house on the night he was journeying back. I would always see him coming towards me. The cat would appear, in front of me, always with a blank indigo background. The image of the cat became magnified and therefore got closer: I didn't see the cat actually walking towards me. This would happen during the hypnogogic state, between sleep and wakefulness: the Alpha state. I got used to linking the cat coming towards me in this manner with seeing him on my doorstep the next morning! This seemed to be a little phase I went through. I found it quite strange to begin with, but just accepted it, and felt happy to know that my cat was safe and well. I suppose I really wondered 'what's going on now?' I had always been used to my dreams coming true after a few weeks, and that was always following a preview of the whole future scenario; now it was a single newsflash about to come true the next day! Maybe I just needed reassurance that my cat was OK! This experience also happened with people I was going to bump into unexpectedly the next day. It doesn't happen so much nowadays, because the person just comes into my mind when I'm awake, and then I bump into them later. My premonition dreams continued, reassuringly!

Warning Dreams with a Telepathic Element

It is possible in a dream to 'become the other person' briefly and to experience what they are experiencing. Mrs M., a seventh-born child, had several premonition dreams, and always knows if her children need help or are in danger. In her dreams, she has the same sensations as the person who is to be involved in the real-life situation. These dreams are of a personal nature, forwarded to me for the purposes of research only, and so I am not including them here.

Dreams in which the dreamer feels they are taking on the other person's reactions are rare when compared to other premonition dreams. If the dream is simultaneous to the actual event, it is more than likely a telepathic dream. If the dream becomes true after several days or more, it is likely to be a premonition dream. The common factor is that the dreamer experiences the feelings and emotions of the person being dreamt about, often having an outsider's view first and then an insider's experience of the (often tragic or traumatic) event. I consider these to be psychic dreams.

Angela Rocker from the West Midlands wrote:

> I dreamt that I was in the passenger seat of a car that was crashing. It was very vivid. I put my hands up to stop my face from being injured, and then I felt the impact. The dream seemed to repeat just that bit. It was by a crossroads, but I was unaware of anything else after the impact. The next morning I told my husband that I felt like I had actually been in the crash – it felt so real. At work, I couldn't stop talking about the crash. Then, when I arrived home, I started to tell my son, but as soon as I mentioned it, he said 'There was a bad accident during the night, just a few hundred yards from our house – by the crossroads.' He handed me the evening paper. On the front page was a picture of a badly mangled car that had hit a lamp-post. The passenger had been injured. Next morning, the girls in the office were saying, 'We saw your accident in the papers last night!' They were all amazed!

Angela also dreamt that some friends were coming back from Australia, even though they had emigrated and were not expected. That day, the couple she had dreamt about were already on their way back, and due to arrive later the same day!

I believe that people who experience the emotions of the third party in a dream are actually clairvoyant and are being communicated with by the victim, indeed may even be undergoing some of their trauma for them, thus alleviating the other person's suffering. This would be considered as spiritual work of an altruistic nature. It is said that some people carry out various types of work to help others at night, during their dream time.

Telepathic Partners

Mrs C. E. Griffith wrote:

> Back in the early seventies, I had been going out with my boyfriend (my future husband) for about six months, when he suddenly finished with me to go out with another girl. I was absolutely devastated, and couldn't stop crying or sleep properly.

The Future in Your Dreams

> During the weeks we'd been apart one of his friends frequently asked me out, but I didn't want to jeopardise my chances of getting back with my ex. After a couple of months passed, I decided to make a new start by going out with the other boy. One Thursday night I made plans to go to a certain pub on Friday, where I knew the lad would be. I would give him a kiss and say he could take me out. After work on Friday I got myself ready to go out with my friends when I had a phone call from my ex-boyfriend, straight out of the blue, after two months. He sounded upset, and wondered if we could meet for a quick drink before I met up with my friends.
>
> I agreed to meet him mostly out of curiosity, I think. He told me he had made a big mistake finishing with me, and that he still loved me and wanted us to get back together. I asked him why, after two months, he had suddenly decided he wanted me back. He then told me how he'd had a dream the night before; that I was in a certain pub, with my friends, when I walked over to his friend, sat on his lap and started kissing him. He said he knew it was only a dream, but it upset him so much because he was worried that it might really happen. This made him realise how he felt about me. I often wonder if I had sent out telepathic messages to him.

Yes, I believe you were both still linked emotionally and telepathically to each other on a deeper level than acquaintances.

A lady who wishes to remain anonymous, from Stonehouse in Gloucestershire, wrote:

> My boyfriend sometimes dated other girls. I always knew when they had split up, because I would dream about it the night before. I would then see him coming back to ask me out again, saying he'd made a mistake! Some people might call this a case of wish-fulfilment, but most of the time I had 'got over it' and wasn't even thinking about him. Sure enough, the very next day, the phone would ring, it would be him, my ex, saying; 'I've made a terrible mistake. We've split up and can I come and see you?'! The dreams included an element of decision-making: I always had a choice of whether I wanted to entertain him or not. They were really dreams telling me that he was available again if I wanted to continue with this somewhat capricious relationship. Yes, I guess I could have foreseen this on the balance of probabilities, but I always got the

timing right! As usual I always took him back because I missed him really!

Lucy B., a beauty therapist from Cheltenham, wrote:

> A few years ago I worked on a ship in Polynesia. I still stayed in close contact with my family as we are all very close. Whilst on the boat, I had a really vivid dream, that my brother's friend's mother (who I knew) was shouting at me and throwing photographs of my brother and I at me! The dream was quite vivid and really quite scary, it made me feel funny all day. The next day, I called my Mum and asked if everything was OK. She told me my brother and his friend had been wrongly accused of something and his friend's Mum's boyfriend attacked my brother. This happened on the same night that I had the dream.

Lucy also had a dream of her grandfather (who is still alive) warning her not to go out with her then boyfriend as he was going to let her down, which he did later on. Lucy felt reassured in her decision to pack him in, having had a dream about it.

Astral Travelling Dreams

During astral travelling in a dream, it is possible to meet up with other people who are still alive as well as people who have died. When we dream like this, we meet up with those who are also travelling in the same astral realms. It is said that the astral realms have seven layers which correspond to different thoughts and activities. These sections have seven colours corresponding to the colours of the rainbow.

Astral travelling in the astral body

Many people have dreamt of flying: human beings have always found this to epitomise freedom, freedom from the confines of time and space, gravitational pull and so on. The idea is that when we are asleep, our soul moves out of the physical body into the astral body and then rests. Our physical and astral bodies are linked by a silver cord coming from the solar plexus. The silver cord stretches, but keeps us connected with our human bodies; this is very important for those travelling long distances in the dream state. If a dreamer is woken up suddenly, the cord pulls them back with a jolt, in the blink of an eye (and the dreamer may feel a bit 'spaced out'). When a person dies the astral cord is either cut or dissolved, freeing the spirit of the person, thus allowing them to go back to their spiritual home, as described in Chapter VI. The astral body is a duplicate of the human form; usually, however, it can alter in appearance in a dream, but, if this happens, the eyes will always be the same, because the eyes are the windows of the soul where a person's true identity resides.

People can go here, there and everywhere in their dreams. Although it is thought that people fly when using astral projection it is also quite possible simply to glide above the ground, walk normally, or hover above the ground as well as flying at great speeds.

Here is a dream from a lady called Jessie:

> I had a dream which seemed rather like 'astral travel'. I don't know where I was going, but my feet never touched the ground. I simply floated, even up and down the stairs. I remember wondering why everyone didn't do this, as it was so much easier than walking!

I too have had many dreams like this. When I was quite young, I was thinking of moving house. Then I dreamt I was travelling along horizontally, seeming just to glide along, until I noticed a close-up view of an old, cracked pavement. Then I became vertical and noticed an old, cracked, dusky red door. The door opened by itself, and I went into the house. I had a look around the rooms, which were quite big. When I looked out of one of the windows, I saw a scrap yard full of old cars. I also noticed that this window was cracked. There was an old lady sitting in a chair in one of the rooms (the large kitchen), but she didn't speak. I quite often meet people in the houses of my dreams. They bear no resemblance to any of the people I know in my waking hours; this is because they are previous inhabitants, who have since gone over to the invisible world.

The following week, my friend asked me if I'd like to move in with her at her new house. I had never been there before (she used to live round the corner from me). I went to visit her, and was looking out of the window when I noticed the scrap yard, full of old cars: yes, and the window had a crack running diagonally. After this recognition, I went to look at the front door. It was painted dusky red, and had the same cracked pavement outside. It was a quaint house, and I spent many happy days there with a very dear friend, making embroideries in the sun and having fun with friends.

While living in this house I had several astral travel experiences. Some were dreams of flying across the town or countryside, but the one which has given me the most faith and encouragement was the one where I experienced a spiritual reunion with my soul group – being at one with those who have always been. Another way my spirit would like to communicate this is to say that I returned to my true home; I was at last reunited with a very special soul group – and what a delight that was. I keep and treasure the memory of this. It gives me a sense of love and peace which is not of this world and it does help to keep me on my journey. Here is an account of what happened:

> The story begins with my evening out in the local tavern, having a dry martini with my friend. No, I wasn't drunk, because I talked so much that I only had one drink all night. My friend remarked that it had been the first time he'd ever been out and only had to buy one drink even though we'd been there for a couple of hours! In short, I had been talking about my life; I felt I was recounting all the events of it, unable to stop. Then we went up the road, my friend went on his way home, and after a cup of warm milk I went to bed. I lay in my bed and thought of my friend walking up the lane. I could see a blue trail following him, winding up the twisting narrow lanes to where he lived. I was preparing to go to sleep, and with half-closed eyes, I turned round on my back to change position. Just then I had an experience whereupon I felt several weights fall upon my body. These I recognised: first was the weight of gravity on my body, being born, then the weight of my personality (although this was quite a light pressure). The next weights came at intervals: I wondered what I had done at these times to merit these 'burdens', as I was now beginning to view them. As I thought this, I was shown the faces of people in the past whom I had hurt emotionally, or transgressed in some way, either wittingly or un-

wittingly. I felt instant regret. When I saw their hurt, I also felt it, in exactly the same way that they had felt it. I was now undergoing the experience that my words and actions had had upon them. This made me feel very uncomfortable: I didn't know how I had affected these people.

Fortunately I had upset only a few people, three that I can recall (it will probably be more now! That's life!). As my body lay heavy on the bed, I thought 'look at the thoughtless way I have behaved'. Then I was filled with a lot of compassion, for myself and the people who had been shown to me. The spirit within me, my spirit, then soared at fantastic speed out of the crown of my head. I became aware at this point that my body was matter, made of the same substance as the furnishings in the room. As I travelled up I was aware of a guardian, holding my hand and taking me somewhere. I could see that my guide was a shining white ethereal colour, and that I was safe.

I entered a realm where there was no sensation of pain or happiness, of birth, life or death. No such thing as time existed here, there was a stillness. There was no language and yet there was communication. I could hear music, but not instrumental: it was the blueprint of music. There was a beautiful harmony of many sounds, but because there is no parallel here, I have to say the nearest would be thousands of voices singing like harp music (believe it or not!) in perfect complex harmony. It was very uplifting, just through being there. We proceeded onwards and upwards. Everything was dark indigo around me.

We travelled more slowly now and I could see the stars, as if out in space. We came to a halt, all was silent; I saw a blue light in the distance. I separated from my guide at this point and floated towards the light. Suddenly I felt a tremendous pull, and was drawn forwards with a great feeling of oneness. In this life it is almost impossible to know what one person thinks or feels unless using telepathy. The body and external situations seem to prevent it, but here in this blissful place, I fitted in. They belonged to me and I belonged to them. I thought about my family and my friends who I had left behind; although we were close, I really didn't miss them at all – it was as if I was in a different world. I knew that I was the missing part of this body of beings, like a jigsaw piece made especially to fit into the design of the whole. Their bodies were a very pale, almost transparent blue and, although separate, they also merged as one. The feeling was one of utter love, joy and completeness, peacefulness and total security. I wanted to stay and became aware of myself; I started to think, 'How did I get here?' I noticed that by that very thought I was beginning to separate from them. I heard a voice saying that I had to go back now. I asked why, then I learnt telepathically what the reason was: I still had to do some work. In a split second the decision had been made and I knew in myself, once it had been shown to me, that it was the right decision.

Next thing, even though I didn't want to go, I found myself going swiftly back into my body again. After considering what had happened I felt happy and relaxed and went to sleep straight away. I told my flat-mate Denise about my experience the next day. I was told I looked glowing and full of radiance for several days later: I felt great! I could still feel the sense of oneness I had experienced for a long time afterwards. I told my friend, 'If this is what it's like to die, it is a very pleasurable experience'. It took away the fear of death for me at that time.

Chapter VIII

The Importance of Sleep

The brain has two main areas which are involved in the sleep process. One makes us go off to sleep, and the other helps us to remain asleep. The first can be set in motion by several factors such as routine, having a darkened bedroom, physical or mental tiredness, and so on. The other is triggered by chemicals in the body and in the brain. Many people feel that sleep is a way of recharging one's batteries – and indeed, research indicates that it is most beneficial to get six hours sleep or more. As with everything else, one is here encouraged to follow one's own rhythm; your body will soon tell you when it feels tired if you pay attention to it! Another theory is that for every hour you sleep before midnight, you receive double the benefit of that sleep, so if you go to bed at 10 p.m. you will awaken feeling more refreshed than if you habitually go to bed after midnight. Further research shows that once you have established a good sleep pattern, you should endeavour to get up at the same time every morning even if it's your weekend off or you had a late night. It's preferable to 'catch up' by going to bed slightly earlier at night.

Dreaming

Sleep plays an important part in the way the body recovers from a day's activity. As well as this, it seems that dreaming clears the circuit, after a busy day of sifting through and analysing a lot of information. Our brain cells manufacture essential chemicals during the dream state which affect intellectual performance during waking hours. If we are deprived of dreams these chemicals are not synthesised, and this has a profound effect in the waking world. Experiments show that if a person is woken up every time they start to dream (this can be detected by observing rapid eye movements, a state known as REM sleep) they will awaken feeling tired; even if they'd had a total of eight hours' sleep, many people reported feeling exhausted, disorientated, agitated and depressed! When the subjects in the dream deprivation experiment started to dream again they showed an increase in their REM dream time. Although the body is resting, the mind in sleep is still active in the dream state; in my opinion, this is because the spirit needs no sleep.

The old barbiturate drugs actually suppressed dreams, which accounted for the unrefreshed groggy feelings associated with taking sleeping pills: 'Barbiturates reduced the profusion of actual eye movements' (from a study by psychiatrist Ian Oswald, 1963); 'If the drugs were administered for one to three weeks, the effects lessened and after they were stopped a rebound increase of REM sleep above normal occurred' (Oswald and Priest, 1965). The rebound was coupled with spontaneous complaints of vivid and unpleasant dreams and also with more than the normal amount of eye movement during REM sleep. However, once the patient stopped taking these drugs, dreams would return to normal. This could take between four and six weeks following the rebound effect; at this time, the brain would tend to overcompensate for the loss of dream time. The same applied to amphetamines, heroin and anti-depressant drugs (of the imipramine type).

There are herbal remedies and aromatherapy oils that help with sleep disturbance, as well as other alternative remedies (such as acupuncture). Dr Keith Hearne has suggested auto-suggestion just before sleep. Using positive affirmations seems to help greatly. (See the bibliography for a list of suggested books.)

Another thing to avoid is excess alcohol, because although this sends one off to sleep initially, the alcohol in the blood system then acts as a stimulant, making the mind more active. One usually wakes up and can't get back to sleep.

It is said that an unbroken good night's sleep prolongs youthful looks. It has been scientifically noticed that the cells in the body regenerate more quickly during this time. Sleep relaxes tired and aching muscles, and tends to press the 'reset button' in general.

A study by psychologists found that people who learn a lot tend to dream a lot. Experiments on rats have shown this. The rats that had to memorise the layout of a maze tended to dream much more than those that didn't. Their REM sleep increased by 50–60 per cent. Once the route became known, the rats' dreaming stages returned to normal!

Chapter IX

Results of Research into Premonition Dreams

Areas Favourable to Premonition Dreams

I believe that, among other things, ley lines may have a bearing on the ability to dream about the future. This is because premonition dreams are more prolific in some areas than others. Ley lines are natural energy lines, which are magnetic and run under the ground. Some ley lines tend to run three abreast, known as three-line leys; these are quite common in the South-West of England, for example this type of ley line runs through the cloisters at Gloucester Cathedral. I find the following quote very interesting!

> Three line Leys [which run together] are fairly common – about 100 metres apart . . . they are found going long ways through churches and long barrows. They have the properties of telepathy when thoughts are focused (as in prayer), and of unconscious healing for both animals and humans. (*The Crop Circle Enigma*, edited by Ralph Noyes, quoting from an essay by farmer Richard G. Andrews, 'The Living Countryside', p. 122)

A lot of the people who wrote to me said that some areas were more favourable to premonition dreams than others, and I too have found this to be the case. Even in the same town, particular areas may be more sensitive than others! Why is this? As mentioned, I think that, among other factors, positive ley lines may have a bearing.

Mr Bernard Berry, in his book *A Lost Roman Road*, explains how he discovered that the Romans used existing ancient roads and sites for their own buildings. So churches, mounds, moats and old farmsteads were found standing not beside, but right on top of, the path of the ancient roads! Ley lines often ended on a mountain peak or a cliff, or a high hill. Hills such as Glastonbury Tor and the Law Hill in Dundee are sited at a convergence of many lines, making these places 'super-spiritual'! Many of the ancient paths contain the names Dod, Merry and Ley (hence the name 'ley lines'). Other old energy line alignments contain the words Red, Black, White, Cole and Cold (see John Mitchell's book *The View over Atlantis* for more information).

In Britain the Druids believe in pathways to new places – portals and doors which lead people into a new time dimension whenever they walk through them. It is believed that yew trees sometimes mark such places. (Two yew trees joining perhaps?) There have been reports of people who accidentally stumble into another time dimension (known as a time-slip). These accounts would make a good subject for another book! Irish folklore often talks of similar tales, usually the result of stumbling across into fairyland. These ancient roads, fairy roads, are known to run along positive ley lines. Circular forms can often be seen where these ley lines cross (usually in the centre), hence the familiar fairy circles, toadstool circles, crop circles, wood circles and so on.

Some esoterics believe that there are earth energies that enable one to tap into the past, present and future. As mentioned above, it is believed that there are natural portals leading from one time dimension into another. For example, the Bermuda Triangle is cited as one such place. The mysterious disappearance of spacecraft in this area is said to be due to a time vortex whisking people and objects into another time dimension. The Triangle is said to be a remainder of the ancient Atlanteans' experiment with time travel. It is thought that a crystal or a device incorporating crystals toppled over when covered by the sea, and that this device is still switched on!

Incidentally, it is well known that convalescent people feel a great benefit from walking along the promenade of Weston-super-Mare near Bristol. This is because the promenade runs over positive ley lines associated with healing and upliftment.

Natural energy lines (ley lines) can be discovered by using a crystal pendulum or dowsing rods and asking (either inwardly to oneself, or out loud) 'Is there an energy line in this area?' Further, 'Is it positive or negative?' According to Richard G. Andrews, a farmer writing in *The Crop Circle Enigma*, crossed rods generally mean a positive line and opening out (opposing) rods indicate negative lines (but see the books mentioned above for more details). Negative ley lines are connected directly to earth energy and are used to discharge other line energies.

Those wishing to have intuitive dreams in any particular house could seek out positive ley energies in a house. It is best to use a

Results of Research into Premonition Dreams

pendulum for this. Suspend the pendulum by one to two inches of chain (if you are right-handed, hold the pendulum in your right hand; use your left hand if left-handed). These questions can then be applied in each of the rooms in turn. First of all, ask the pendulum to show you the sign for 'Yes', and then the sign for 'No'. Typically the pendulum will begin to move, apparently of its own accord, in circles or strokes, to indicate the answer. You may then walk around the room with your pendulum – it will swing in the 'Yes' movement when it comes across a line of energy. Alternatively, you may choose simply to stand in the middle, and with the other arm outstretched, point your finger at the floor (or walls if you prefer) and slowly turn your body in a circular motion saying 'Is there an energy line in this room?' The pendulum will start swinging when it comes across an energy line. If nothing happens, or you get a 'No' sign, there is no ley line there. If you do get a 'Yes' response, ask 'Is this vibration going to have a good influence on me?' and, for those wishing to dream of the future, 'Is this room conducive to premonition dreams?'

Having determined whether the room is suitable for dreaming about the future, you can now use a colour spectrum chart. This is used in conjunction with the pendulum. Hold the pendulum over each colour in turn until it begins to swing 'Yes'. This is the colour most beneficial for you at this time. If, for instance, the colour is yellow, one could imagine the colour yellow filling the room, in order to stimulate dreams about the future. Or just place a yellow pillowcase on your pillow. As with all exercises like this, it is recommended by experienced dowsers that you use psychic protection. To do this, imagine yourself inside your car, concealed by a fabulous white light; or cover yourself in an imaginary intensely bright bubble of white or golden light which you would visualise as a protective shield; or imagine yourself inside a solid ball of either blue, violet or gold light. Try each method to find which one resonates with you best. Another important method is to say a prayer for protection and wear a religious symbol that means something to you, for example an even-sided cross. Believers hold that this will ensure an accurate and safe response from the pendulum. The Victorians liked to place embroidered prayers and religious pictures above their beds to promote a good night's sleep, for similar reasons.

Some people like to use crystals to help bring about helpful dreams. It is said that dried lavender, Herkimer diamonds and

The Future in Your Dreams

amethyst are good for stimulating futuristic dreams. Crystal experts would also recommend indicolite (blue tourmaline), blue kyanite, celestite, and moonstone at the time of a full moon. These would have to be placed by your bed at night or, for a stronger effect, underneath your pillow. For greater clarity one can add jade with clear needlepoint quartz to the above crystals. Keep a dream diary beside your bed to record your dreams. For those who have nightmares or troublesome dreams, then jet, topaz or pink mangnao calcite are strongly recommended, again to be placed beneath the pillow, or beside or beneath the bed.

The late Sir Mortimer Wheeler suggested that the Romano-British temple discovered at Lydney in Gloucestershire was in fact designed as a healing temple complete with abatons. An abaton was a very special room where people would envoke an answer in a dream.

Modern researchers are now exploring the evocative and healing powers of such places in Britain. Volunteers offer to sleep at sacred sites. During the night, after they have shown signs of dreaming, a researcher wakes them to record the details of their dream. It is hoped that when enough experiments have been undertaken a significant pattern of experiences related to sites will emerge.

The results of my own survey indicate that the main areas of premonition dreams which readers wrote to me about were as follows:

- Scotland: Glasgow, Falkirk, Aberdeen, Carnoustie, Dundee, Edinburgh
- Ireland: Dublin and Belfast
- England, North-East: Newcastle, Tynemouth, South Shields, Sunderland, Durham, Darlington
- England, Northern and Eastern: Leeds, Pontefract, Barnsley, Sheffield, Rochdale, Pickering, Peterborough, Lincolnshire, Lincoln, Cleethorpes, Grimsby, Hull
- England, North-West: Manchester, Liverpool, Blackpool
- England, Midlands: Derby, Birmingham, Coventry, Stafford, Stourport on Severn (Worcs.), Stourbridge (W. Midlands), Wolverhampton, Stoke-on-Trent
- Wales: Aberyswyth, Llandudno, Wrexham, Clwyd
- England, South-West: Tewkesbury, Cheltenham, Bristol, Weston-super-Mare, Bath, Chippenham, Devon, Penzance

Results of Research into Premonition Dreams

- England, South: Oxford, Amesbury, Cambridge, Canterbury, Lewes, Chichester, Sussex, Suffolk, Tonbridge, Kent, Chelmsford, Maidenhead, Chessington, Hampshire, Portsmouth, London.

Anyone who pinpoints these areas on a map might find it interesting to see if a pattern emerges (I managed to draw diagonal lines)! In short, the areas above are the general areas revealed to me where dreaming about a future event occurred. Of course, other factors play a part, such as the current emotional state of the dreamer; premonition dreams will come and be remembered when needed.

For other results from the questionnaire please see the charts at the end of the book.

The results also show that a high number of women with these experiences of dreams about future events were born on an astrological cusp. A cusp is that area between one astrological sign and the next, and usually spans two days on either side of each sign. Research by the scientist Dr Keith Hearne, who is interested in precognitive and premonition dreams, suggests that women born on or around a full moon are more likely to have premonition dreams than those who were not. This could be because the moon controls the tides and other fluids; perhaps this 'pull of the full moon event' stimulates certain parts of the brain which would not otherwise have been stimulated. (I myself was born around the time of a full moon on New Year's Day.)

Strangely enough, although it is often said that those born under the water signs of the zodiac are most intuitive, I found that actually the fire signs and earth signs were quite high scorers in this department! (I know it all depends on the other aspects in a person's chart, but I just thought I'd mention it anyway.) It is thought that psychic skills could be hereditary, hence the saying 'A seventh daughter of a seventh daughter, or seventh son of a seventh son'. I have certainly noticed a tendency for psychic abilities to run in families. In my own family, my great-grandmother used to have dreams about the future which later came true, and both my sisters are very intuitive although they might prefer to call this the gift of knowledge or discernment. Some of the women who wrote to me came from families in which more than one person would have extrasensory perception in general. They may not all have had dreams about the future, but they would have had a 'sixth sense' about things.

People who were psychic as children often do not reveal their gifts until adulthood. Psychic skills can be dismissed by some as pure fantasy, while charlatans only add fuel to this notion! Many people have experienced reproach by those who are afraid of the unknown. These fearful others, who seem to use five senses and logic only, choose not to acknowledge information gleaned by people who operate on the Alpha level of thinking. At the Alpha level, the brain bypasses the logical thought processes (on the right side of the brain) and utilises the creative thought processes (left side of brain). There are now courses on this subject, led by Colin Clark. Colin, who is an expert in this field, tells how he believes that psychic ability is natural, and thinks everyone can tap into it to some degree. (Please see the bibliography, under 'Further Information', for more details.)

Most people, even sceptics, can access the Alpha state. Those people who do use the Alpha levels actually tend to be very successful in life, because they are paying attention to their heightened intuition, and eventually become guided by it to their benefit.

Common Factors Between Dreamers

The ability to dream about the future is cross-cultural, and has no social boundaries. The people who took part in my research were of all ages and from all walks of life. They came across in their writing as being warm, caring, witty and articulate. They were also sociable and active, as shown by their willingness to take part in this questionnaire.

Of the people who wrote to me, 93 per cent had a preview of an actual event that later came to pass. The remaining 7 per cent had symbolic dreams that also came true.

Some of the women took dream interpretations from books. However, most tended to interpret their own symbols. I have found this to be the case myself. It really doesn't matter if your premonition dreams are partly symbolic and partly true to life as long as you recognise them as being premonition dreams containing information pertaining to the future.

Some 73 per cent of the people who wrote to me said that their premonition dreams were very vivid and made such an impression that they could still remember those dreams for several days, even weeks, later. In fact these dreams do remain with people for years, even a lifetime. This is because it is quite astonishing when they come true, and the dream is underlined somehow in the memory, just as with any unforgettable experience, such as getting married or falling in love.

The average number of premonition dreams per dreamer was five (see the charts for fuller details).

Some people's dreams would come true on the same day as the dream (on waking); others came true several weeks later. There were very few people who dreamt regularly of a future event.

Around 28 per cent had flying dreams of travelling into the future; 68 per cent also had other psychic experiences such as out-of-body experiences and déjà vu. The experience of déjà vu can indicate a past life memory, or it could point to the memory of a premonition dream. It could also be due to a neurological effect, of remembering what you just saw a split second ago (the messages in the brain being momentarily out of synchronisation). It is for you to decide, but I think that if you have the feelings of already knowing a place and reacting to it on an emotional level, then you could be experiencing soul recognition, as opposed to brain recognition.

Astral travel, flying dreams and out-of-body experiences are all terms for the same thing: the astral body leaving the physical body, while still connected to the material body via an astral cord.

Some people saw ghosts or met dead relatives in dreams, which they mostly found helpful and a comfort. Usually this would occur on the astral level, but some people saw, and talked to, these spirits while still awake. Some people would smell a particular scent and then think about a person who would once have worn that same perfume. This would be a more subtle level of communication, one where the spirit of the dead person, not wishing to alarm the recipient, still wants to reassure them that there is more to life than meets the eye.

It is interesting to note that in 1936 the Archbishop of Canterbury, Cosmo Lang, appointed a commission of eleven distinguished church men and women to decide whether 'communication with the dead' could be taken seriously by the Church of England. In 1939, the commission reported that 'Claims of Spiritualism are probably true, and [that] there is nothing that contradicts the beliefs of Christianity'. The report was released in March 1979.

Of the respondents to my questionnaire, 51 per cent had telepathic experiences. When using telepathy, a person is able to communicate with another person or animal, without talking, and without having to be physically present.

I had a telepathic dream once in which an ancient apple tree communicated with me. The tree had a strong and beautiful voice. In the dream the tree showed me that it was about to die. Dead leaves were falling into a river I was standing in. The river had been free-flowing, but now I had come to the end of it and there was only a sheer bank ahead of me, one that I couldn't climb because it was too steep. I was wading through the leaves from the apple tree. Then the tree put one of its branches into the water and said 'I will help you'. I held on to the branch and it lifted me up on to the riverbank, covered in leaves. I felt grateful to the tree, and felt that the tree was glad to help before it died. I woke up feeling greatly strengthened. Three days later I came home from shopping, and the Old Keswick apple tree had been chopped down. A new road was soon built there in its place.

Of the people who wrote to me, 91 per cent were brought up in a religious environment (Christian); 41 per cent still followed their religion by going to church. Of the 91 per cent, all still believed in God and a higher order than ourselves, because of their experiences. Of the others, 7 per cent were agnostics, 2 per cent were atheists.

Some 70 per cent of the respondents believed in reincarnation. Rev. Lesley Weatherhead from the Methodist Church investigated the possibility of reincarnation within Christianity, and published a book about it. I mention this because some people believe that their dreams may be recollections of a past life in which they revisit familiar places.

> The disciples said 'Why do the scribes say that Elijah must come first [before the Messiah]?' And Jesus answered saying, 'Elijah has already come'. Then the disciples understood that He spoke to them of John the Baptist. (Matthew, ch. 17 v. 12)

Reincarnation was a common idea for people around the time of Jesus, and it is not denied or criticised anywhere in the New

Testament. The early church accepted this until the Council of Constantinople in AD 553, who then discarded it by one vote (3 to 2) in *Contra Celsus* and *De Principilis*.

A person's diet did not seem to affect the ability to dream about the future. Of all the respondents only 15 per cent were vegetarians.

Some 10 per cent did yoga, which is known to enhance one's spirituality. When I was younger I found that I was much more intuitive after only a few months of practising Hatha Yoga exercises every day for thirty minutes.

All yoga practices will teach the belief in chakras and the need for chakra balancing. It is commonly thought that the body has energy centres or chakras, with each chakra governing particular physical and emotional states. The third eye or brow chakra enables some people to see hidden spiritual truths. When attuned to this state, it is possible to access the past, present and future, preferably (at least initially) under the guidance of a spiritual teacher.

Reactions

Many of the dreamers said they felt shocked and stunned when they realised that they had just dreamt of a future event. This changed to feelings of intrigue, reassurance and acceptance, once the initial shock had settled down!

Other people (not so common) recorded feelings of elation and exhilaration on waking from a premonition dream, feeling happy and special because they had been shown a glimpse of the future. Generally the initial response was a 'double take': 'Can this really be happening?' Once accustomed to the dreams most people looked forward to having some more.

Some 33 per cent said they were able to act on the information given in a premonition dream. These people were able to remember the premonition dream and to do some 'quick thinking' before the event occurred, thus avoiding the outcome as shown in the dream. They neither paused to mull over the message nor sought the advice of others; they just acted immediately, and it paid off.

The remaining 67 per cent were unable to act on the information shown in a dream about a future event. Most people will take in an impression of what is about to happen and will then fail to act. This is due either to forgetting until reminded by the experience, or to feeling unable to act because of logical reasoning overriding an (often bizarre) idea or hunch. Another common experience was that of the dreamer observing an event not directly related to them. They may have foreseen a news event or an accident involving people unknown to them, or the time lapse between the dream and the actual event may have been too long for them to remain constantly vigilant. These results bring up questions about free will and predestination.

Free Will versus Predestination

If you can see the future in your dreams does this mean that the whole of your destiny has in fact already been mapped out for you, regardless of any input on your part?

The doctrine of free will asserts that people are free to make choices affecting their own destiny and moral behaviour. 'I act freely' means 'I would have done otherwise if I had chosen to do so'.

The doctrine of predestination states that all the events of a person's life are predetermined. There is a cause, therefore an effect will follow.

These two theories can be reconciled by the notion that, yes, our lives are pre-planned – however, we can either follow along this original plan or we can choose to alter our destiny by the use of free will and action. Acceptance of this apparent paradox requires the reader to understand the notion of soul and rebirth. An interesting book which covers life between lives is Michael Newton's *Journey of Souls*. Dr Newton used hypnosis techniques to regress some of his patients, and discovered that the soul is shown a preview of the next incarnation before being born. They also meet the key players in their lives, whom they will recognise. In life, sometimes a particular object, such as a gift received, will trigger the recognition of the key player. Sometimes a party triggers the memory of the pre-arranged meeting at the appointed time. Some people call these a divine appointment, because the two people concerned will be very tuned in to each other and may well already have a lot in common on many different levels! This is because everybody on Earth has a reason for being here. Sometimes we miss the cues and clues when meeting our soulmates, or when keeping our divine appointments. In this case we live the alternative path, learning the same lessons until we can eventually join the original path again. For many, this would be the path of harmony and true fulfilment.

Hindus believe that the original life path chosen by the soul is not necessarily the easiest or the wealthiest, or even the happiest. This is because of the law of karma, and karmic debt.

Both St Augustine and St Francis of Assisi believed in reincarnation. With reincarnation comes the notion of karma. The interaction between the universe and an individual, or between one person and another, creates a set of circumstances which some call karma. These circumstances can be blindly followed or can be altered, by the use of our mind, determination and free will. The belief goes like this: what one does in this life has consequences – you will reap what you sow, either in this lifetime or in another lifetime. Whatever effects you caused will have to be addressed next time round! If you lead a good life you come back in a nice environment with nice happy people, or you will go to the spiritual planes, to spend time with God. If you lead a selfish and ignorant life, you may come back to a difficult life where you confront those people you once hurt and you will have to work hard to redress the balance. If you don't want to meet, in another lifetime, these people with whom you have had a problem, then it is a good idea to forgive them now and let go of them. I know this may sound difficult. To forgive is not to condone, but to disentangle yourself from any further influence from that person. Disengage, by using forgiveness.

The Cause of Premonition Dreams

Since premonition dreams always come before the actual event, it seems we can rule out chance. Physical causes such as eating cheese or spicy food could bring about certain types of dreams; however, this does not trigger premonition dreams. It seems that the most popular beliefs are that the soul is eternal, without beginning and without end; we are travellers here for a short time only, and when we die we will return to our spiritual home, where time is infinite.

Some of us are able to gain insights into the future by means as yet scientifically unknown. Psychics suggest that we get messages from a higher source, for example from God, spiritual guides/angels, our deceased relatives, or simply from our higher selves. During astral travelling, the astral body can contact the living and the dead. Some people can control this consciously, but most people just go there without effort as part of the dream, while sleeping. Some psychologists think that to be able to travel through time and space in a dream state is a natural ability.

The ancient Greeks knew about two types of time: Chronos (chronological time), which is calculated in seconds, minutes, hours, days and years, and Cairos, meaning timeless moments. Premonition dreams occur during the latter time dimension. Synchronistic events occur because telepathic people can tap into a kind of Internet or pool of current opinions. It is generally held by most psychic researchers and esoterics that past, present and future all co-exist and belong within eternity – the never-ending now, the timeless zone!

Scientific Research

I would now like to include the following scientific research into personal factors affecting premonition abilities; here are excerpts from a few psychology journals, held at the University of Oxford.
Jefferson N. C. McFarland said:

> There is strong support for the assumption of high psychic ability correlating with social and personality factors. (*Parapsychology Journal*, 1990, p. 170)

This is backed up by my own research, i.e. that outgoing, open-minded people tend to have more premonition dreams than other personality types.

> It is my belief that many mentally retarded children rely upon extrasensory perception, as they do not always find the normal channels of communication all that easy.

On a personal note of interest, I was born in Ireland, and I learnt English for the first year and a half of my life; then my parents moved to South America and I had to learn to speak in Spanish. During this time, I believe I developed a heightened level of intuition. After a year of virtual silence, I began to speak in fluent Spanish, and my talents of extrasensory perception began. I found I was able to 'read' people without speaking to them, just through observation. My sister and I had a native South American Indian nanny, who did not find any of my supernatural experiences at all strange. I was very creative at school in Argentina, and I actually drew pictures reminiscent of hills in the Stroud valleys, which I had the privilege to view, in real life, many years later.

Creativity often relates to high psychic scores, but this relation may be due only to common personality variables, such as openness and spontaneity. These are qualities that I, and the people who wrote to me, all shared in common. Many of the people who took part in my questionnaire had creative hobbies.

Conclusion

As mentioned earlier, as a result of my research and because of personal experience, I would say that the main reason for premonition dreams (that is, looking into the distant future) is because some of us are able to access and recall information from another time dimension, kept within the timeless zone. In the dream state, we are able to access past, present and future, all at the same time; there is no time division. Because of this, we find that we can clearly predict the future. Dreaming about the future is an ancient art. The mystery still remains as to why the dreamtime portals into the future are open to us on some occasions and not on others.

The Ancient Greeks believed there were two gates leading to dreams. One set of gates was made of ivory and was presided over by an elephant with large ivory tusks; the other set of gates was made of horn, and was presided over by a cow with beautiful horns. The Gates of Ivory led to fictional dreams, but the Gates of Horn led to futuristic dreams – dreams which later came true. This book gives examples of those who have travelled through time, and space, perhaps even through the horned gates! And so we journey on, towards our Gates of Dreams.

APPENDIX

Charts

TIME BETWEEN DREAM AND ACTUAL EVENT

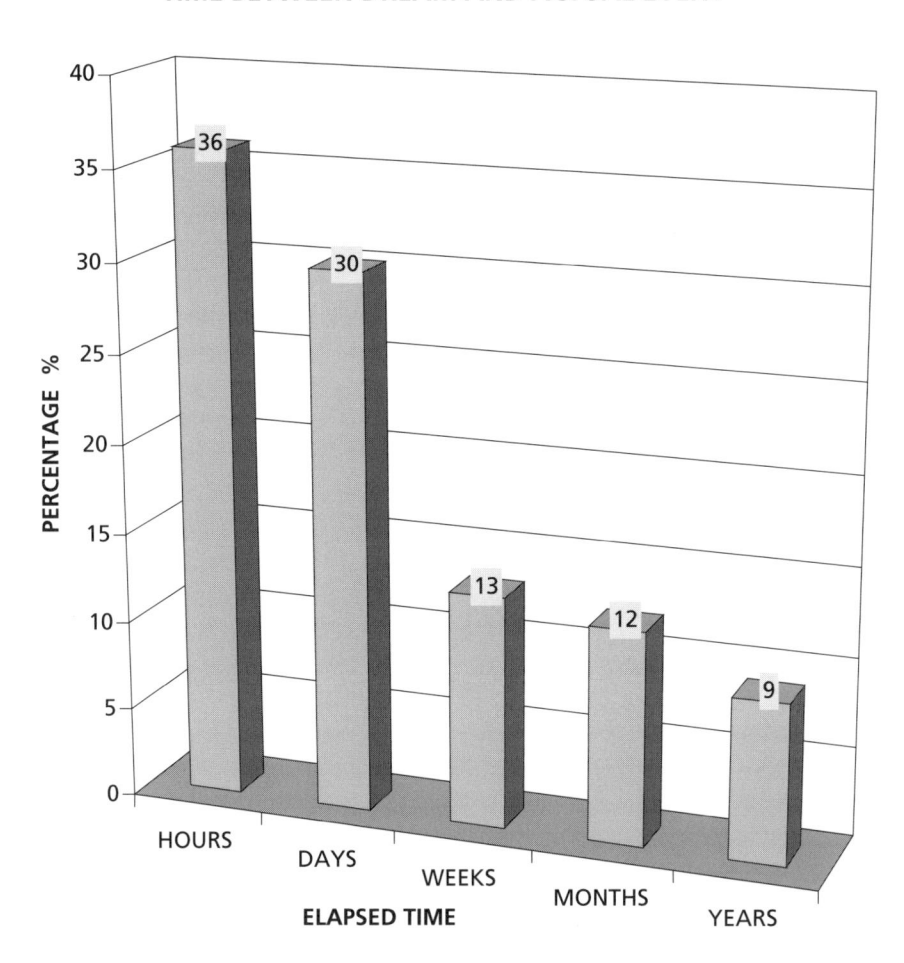

ELAPSED TIME	PERCENTAGE %
HOURS	36
DAYS	30
WEEKS	13
MONTHS	12
YEARS	9

The Future in Your Dreams

REACTING TO WARNINGS

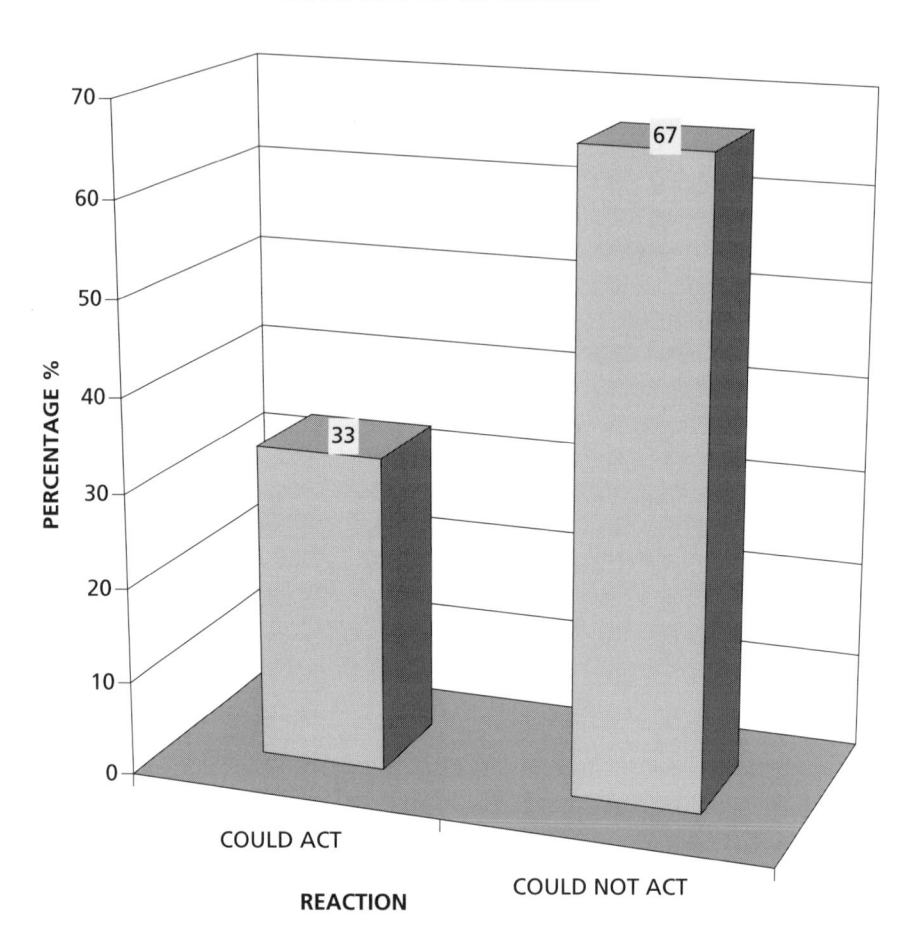

Charts

DREAMS AND OTHER EXPERIENCES

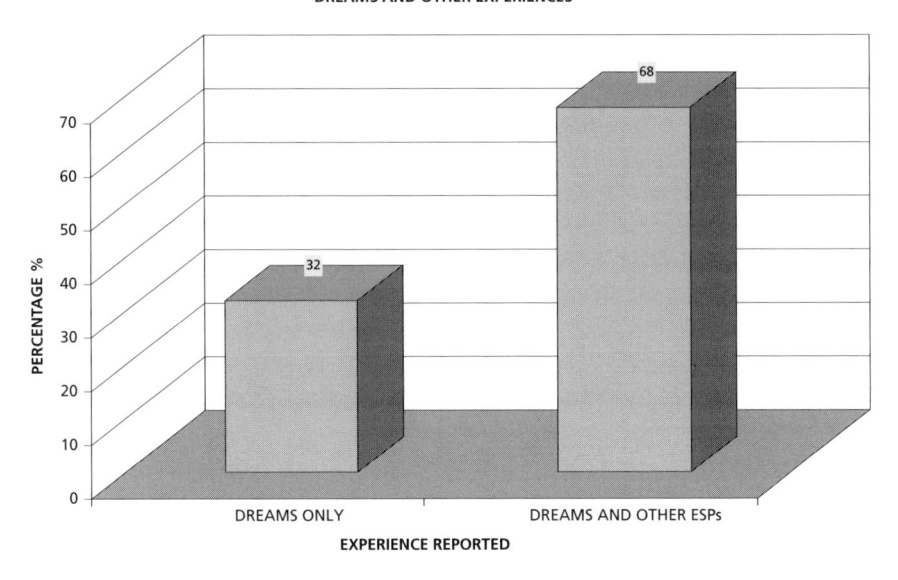

The Future in Your Dreams

ADDITIONAL EXPERIENCES OF PROPHETIC DREAMERS
(Please note: experiences can fall in to more than one category)

EXPERIENCE REPORTED	PERCENTAGE %
TELEPATHY	51
DÉJÀ VU	8
OUT OF BODY	27
CLAIRVOYANCE	47

Charts

NUMBER OF RESPONDENTS REPORTING MORE THAN ONE PREMONITION DREAM

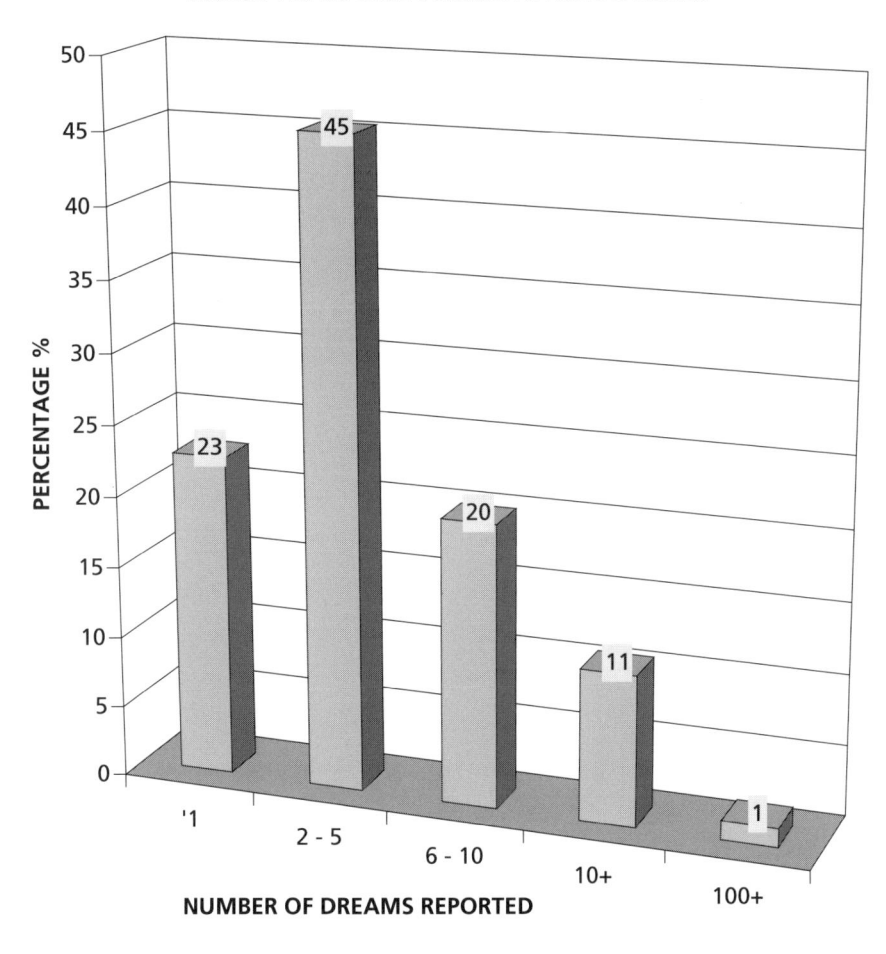

Number of Dreams Reported	Percentage %
1	23
2 - 5	45
6 - 10	20
10+	11
100+	1

ORDER OF BIRTH OF RESPONDENTS

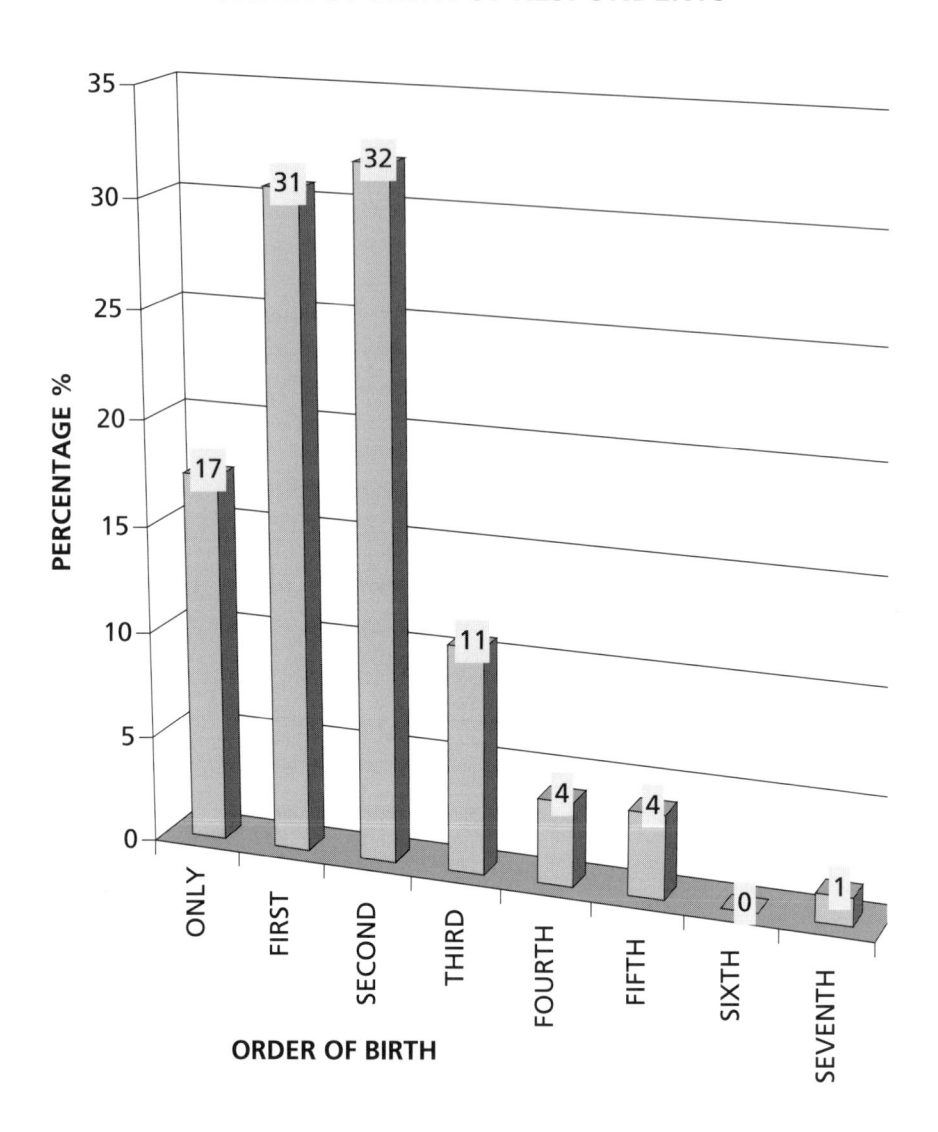

Order of Birth	Percentage %
ONLY	17
FIRST	31
SECOND	32
THIRD	11
FOURTH	4
FIFTH	4
SIXTH	0
SEVENTH	1

Bibliography

Books Which Might Be of Interest

Altman, Jack: *1001 Dreams (An Illustrated Guide To Dreams and Their Meanings)*. Duncan Baird Ltd, London. 2002.
Baigent, Michael: *The Jesus Papers*. Element, London. 2006.
Bates, Brian: *The Way of Wyrd*. Hay House, London. 1983.
Berry, B.: *A Lost Roman Road*. George Allen & Unwin, London. 1953.
Borrow, George: *Romano Lovo-Lil. A Book of the Gypsy*. Alan Smith, Gloucester. 1982.
Brinkley, Dannion: *Saved by the Light*. Piatkus Books Ltd, London. 2005.
Carr-Gomm, Philip: *The Druid Way*. Element, London, revised Shaftsbury. 1993.
Carter, Mary Ellen and Cayce, Hugh Lynn: *Edgar Cayce on Prophecy*. Warner Books, New York. 1968.
Cavendish, Richard: *Unsolved Mysteries Of The Universe*. Treasure Press, London. 1987.
Covenly, Peter and Highfield, Roger: *The Arrow of Time*. Flamingo, London. 1991.
Devereux, Paul: *The New Leyhunters Guide*. Gothic Image Publications, Glastonbury, Somerset. 1994.
Fenwick, Peter and Elizabeth: *The Truth In the Light*. Headline Book Publishing, London. 1995.
Fisher, J. and Commins, P. (eds): *Predictions*. Sidgwick and Jackson, London. 1981.
Gascoine, Bamber: *The Christians*. Granada Publishing Ltd, London. 1980.
Guiley, Rosemary E.: *Encyclopedia Of Angels*. Facts On File Books, New York. 1996.
Hawking, Stephen: *A Brief History of Time*. Bantam Books, London. 1997.
Hearne, Keith and Melbourne, David: *Understanding Dreams*. New Holland Publishers, London. 1999.
Hogue, John: *The Millennium Book of Prophecy*. Harper, San Francisco. 1994.

Holzer, Hans: *The Psychic Side Of Dreams*. St Paul, Minnesota. 1992.

Hope, Murry: *Practical Techniques of Psychic Self-Defence*. The Aquarian Press (Thornsons Publishing Group), Wellingborough, Northamptonshire. 1983.

Jacobi, Jolande: *The Psychology of C.G. Jung*. Routledge & Kegan Paul, London. 1951.

Lee, S.G.M. and Mayes, A.R. (eds): *Dreams and Dreaming*. Penguin Education, Penguin Books Ltd, Harmondsworth. 1974.

Mauleverer, W.: *Twelve Great Sayings of the Mystics*. Arthur James, Worcester. 1955.

Medina, John: *The Clock of Ages*. Cambridge University Press, Cambridge. 1996.

Mitchell, John: *The View over Atlantis*. Abacus, London. 1973.

Moody, Raymond A.: *Life After Life*. Mockingbird Books, Georgia, USA. 1977.

Moody, Raymond A.: *Life Before Life: Regressions into Past Lives*. Macmillan, London. 1990.

Neusner, J., Frerichs, S., Virgil, P. and Flesher, M. (eds): *Religion, Science and Magic*. Oxford University Press, Oxford. 1989.

Newton, Michael: *Destiny of Souls*. Llewelyn Press, St Paul, Minnesota. 1994.

Newton, Michael: *Journey of Souls*. Llewelyn Press, St Paul, Minnesota. 2005.

Noyes, Ralph (ed.): *The Crop Circle Enigma*. Gateway Books, London. 1991.

Oswald, Ian: *Sleep and Waking*. Elsevier Ltd, London. 1962.

Seymour, P.A.H.: *The Birth of Christ: Exploding the Myth*. Virgin Publishing, London. 1998.

Snow, Chet B.: *Dreams Of The Future*. Aquarian Press, London. 1991.

Tanner, Wilda B.: *The Mystical Magical Marvelous World of Dreams*. Sparrow Hawk Press, Oklahoma. 1993.

Van de Castle, R. L., in Lee, S.G.M. and Mayes, A.R. (eds): *Dreams and Dreaming*. Penguin Education, Penguin Books Ltd, Harmondsworth. 1974.

Weatherhead, Lesley: *The Case For Reincarnation (A Lecture Given To The City Temple Literary Society)*. M.C. Peto, London. 1978.

Wegner, G.S.: *6000 Years of the Bible*. Hodder & Stoughton, London. 1963.

Wilson, Colin: *Mysteries*. Watkins Publishing, New York. 2006.

Wilson, Colin and Grant, John: *The Directory of Possibilities*. Web & Bower, Exeter. 1981.

Woods, R. (ed.): *The World of Dreams*. Random House, London. 1947.

Parapsychology Journals and Papers

Abstracts and Papers from the 33rd Annual Convention. Institute for Parapsychology, College Station, Durham.

Barret, Deirdre: 'Flying Dreams and Lucidity: An Empirical Study of Their Relationship', *Dreaming*, vol. 1, no. 2 (1991), p. 11. (Psychical Research Library).

Jefferson, N. C. McFarland: 'Matches and Mismatches', *Parapsychology Journal*, vol. 1 (1990), p. 170.

Kanthamani, H.: 'Psychic Ability Among Youth', *Research in Parapsychology*, vol. 33 (1990), p. 151. (Abstract from 33rd Annual Convention.)

Oswald, I., Berger, R.J., Jaramillo, R.A., Keddie, K.M.G., Olley, P.C., and Blunkett, G.B.: 'Human Brain Protein, Drugs and Dreams', *Nature*, vol. 223 (1969), pp. 893–7.

Oswald, I.: 'Melancholia and Barbiturates: A Controlled EEG, Body And Eye Movement Study of Sleep', *British Journal of Psychiatry*, vol. 109 (1963), pp. 66–78.

Oswald, I. and Priest, R.G.: 'Five Weeks to Escape the Sleeping Pill Habit', *British Medical Journal*, vol. 2 (1965), pp. 1093–9.

Further Information

If you want to share your dreams about a future world event, you might like to try the Central Premonitions Registry:

Society for Psychical Research
49 Marloes Road
London
W8 6LA
Website: www.spr.ac.uk.

For accounts of spiritual and religious experiences see:
www.alisterhardyreligiousexperience.co.uk

The Future in Your Dreams

Sir Alister Hardy founded the Religious Experience Research Centre at Manchester College, Oxford University in 1969.

If you would like to know more about psychic abilities and whether they are natural or supernatural, and how to access the Alpha state, look up Colin Clark's website:
www.drawinward.com

The dream research carried out at sacred sites was at one time organised by Sir Mortimer Wheeler and volunteers, under the name 'The Dragon Project'. Current contact details are unavailable.

For permission to quote from their sources, acknowledgement is made to the following:
Dr Peter Fenwick, co-author of *The Truth in the Light* (Headline Book Publishing. 1995) and Dr Raymond A. Moody, author of *Life After Life* (Mockingbird Books, Georgia, USA. 1977)